WORLD BANK STAFF WORKING PAPERS
Number 577

MANAGEMENT AND DEVELOPMENT SERIES
Number 4

Managing State-Owned Enterprises

Mary M. Shirley

The World Bank
Washington, D.C., U.S.A.

This is a working document published informally by the World Bank. To present the results of research with the least possible delay, the typescript has not been prepared in accordance with the procedures appropriate to formal printed texts, and the World Bank accepts no responsibility for errors. The publication is supplied at a token charge to defray part of the cost of manufacture and distribution.

The World Bank does not accept responsibility for the views expressed herein, which are those of the authors and should not be attributed to the World Bank or to its affiliated organizations. The findings, interpretations, and conclusions are the results of research supported by the Bank; they do not necessarily represent official policy of the Bank. The designations employed, the presentation of material, and any maps used in this document are solely for the convenience of the reader and do not imply the expression of any opinion whatsoever on the part of the World Bank or its affiliates concerning the legal status of any country, territory, city, area, or of its authorities, or concerning the delimitation of its boundaries, or national affiliation.

The full range of World Bank publications, both free and for sale, is described in the *Catalog of Publications*; the continuing research program is outlined in *Abstracts of Current Studies*. Both booklets are updated annually; the most recent edition of each is available without charge from the Publications Sales Unit, Department T, The World Bank, 1818 H Street, N.W., Washington, D.C. 20433, U.S.A., or from the European Office of the Bank, 66 avenue d'Iéna, 75116 Paris, France.

When this paper was first published Mary M. Shirley was a senior economist with the Projects Advisory Staff of the World Bank.

Library of Congress Cataloging in Publication Data

```
Shirley, Mary M., 1945-
   Managing state-owned enterprises.

   (World Bank staff working papers ; no. 577. Management
and development subseries ; no. 4)
   Bibliography: p.
   1. Government business enterprises--Management.
I. Title.  II. Series: World Bank staff working papers ;
no. 577.  III. Series: World Bank staff working papers.
Management and development subseries ; no. 4.
HD62.35.S54  1983        351.009'2      83-14770
ISBN 0-8213-0241-8
```

Abstract

State-owned enterprises (SOEs) are increasingly important actors in developing economies, and more and more attention has been focused on how to enhance their operating efficiency. This paper suggests ways to improve SOE efficiency by examining on the special circumstances and constraints that are common to most of them. These include confused and conflicting objectives; government intervention in operating decisions; monopoly powers; and managers who are not held accountable for results or given the incentives to perform well, and whose skills are inappropriate for a commercial enterprise. Although all of these problems are complex and resistant to change, many countries have begun to develop useful approaches to correct some of the main weaknesses of SOEs. Negotiated agreements between governments and SOEs are used to clarify objectives and set targets for both parties. Systems to monitor and evaluate performance take into account the special constraints placed on SOEs and adjust for distorted prices. Competition and better accountability to customers are used to encourage efficiency. Incentives linked to performance help motivate top managers. Compensation and training can be geared toward creating a corps of competent managers with appropriate skills. Finally, governments are reducing the managerial and fiscal burden of SOEs through selective liquidation and divestiture.

Acknowledgments

The author gratefully acknowledges helpful comments on earlier drafts by Ramgopal Agarwala, Jonathan Brown, David Burke, Richard Heaver, Leroy Jones, Frans Kok, Geoffrey Lamb, Pierre Landell-Mills, Martin Schrenk, David Williams, and Peter Wright.

Papers in the Management and Development Series

Agarwala, Ramgopal. Price Distortions and Growth in Developing Countries. World Bank Staff Working Paper no. 575.

Agarwala, Ramgopal. Planning in Developing Countries: Lessons of Experience. World Bank Staff Working Paper no. 576.

Cochrane, Glynn. Policies for Strengthening Local Government in Developing Countries. World Bank Staff Working Paper no. 582.

Gordon, David. Development Finance Companies, State and Privately Owned: A Review. World Bank Staff Working Paper no. 578.

Gould, David J., and Jose A. Amaro-Reyes. The Effects of Corruption on Administrative Performance: Illustrations from Developing Countries. World Bank Staff Working Paper no. 580.

Knight, Peter T. Economic Reform in Socialist Countries: The Experiences of China, Hungary, Romania, and Yugoslavia. World Bank Staff Working Paper no. 579.

Kubr, Milan, and John Wallace. Successes and Failures in Meeting the Management Challenge: Strategies and Their Implementation. World Bank Staff Working Paper no. 585.

Lethem, Francis J., and Lauren Cooper. Managing Project-Related Technical Assistance: The Lessons of Success. World Bank Staff Working Paper no. 586.

Ozgediz, Selcuk. Managing the Public Service in Developing Countries: Issues and Prospects. World Bank Staff Working Paper no. 583.

Paul, Samuel. Training for Public Administration and Management in Developing Countries: A Review. World Bank Staff Working Paper no. 584.

Rondinelli, Dennis A., John R. Nellis, and G. Shabbir Cheema. Decentralization in Developing Countries: A Review of Recent Experience. World Bank Staff Working Paper no. 581.

Shinohara, Miyohei, Toru Yanagihara, and Kwang Suk Kim. The Japanese and Korean Experiences in Managing Development. Ed. Ramgopal Agarwala. World Bank Staff Working Paper no. 574.

Shirley, Mary M. Managing State-Owned Enterprises. World Bank Staff Working Paper no. 577.

Foreword

This study is one in a series of World Bank Staff Working Papers devoted to issues of development management. Prepared as background papers for the World Development Report 1983, they provide an in-depth treatment of the subjects dealt with in Part II of the Report. The thirteen papers cover topics ranging from comprehensive surveys of management issues in different types of public sector institutions (for example, state-owned enterprises, the public service, and local government agencies) to broad overviews of such subjects as planning, management training, technical assistance, corruption, and decentralization.

The central concern underlying these papers is the search for greater efficiency in setting and pursuing development goals. The papers focus on the role of the state in this process, stress the importance of appropriate incentives, and assess the effectiveness of alternative institutional arrangements. They offer no general prescriptions, as the developing countries are too diverse--politically, culturally, and in economic resources-- to allow the definition of a single strategy.

The papers draw extensively on the experiences of the World Bank and other international agencies. They were reviewed by a wide range of readership from developing and developed countries inside and outside the Bank. They were edited by Victoria Macintyre. Rhoda Blade-Charest, Banjonglak Duangrat, Jaunianne Fawkes, and Carlina Jones prepared the manuscripts for publication.

I hope that these studies will be useful to practitioners and academicians of development management around the world.

Pierre Landell-Mills
Staff Director
World Development Report 1983

Acronyms

BIM	Board of Industrial Management (Pakistan)
BPE	Bureau of Public Enterprises (India)
CDF	Charbounages de France
CEO	chief executive officer
CGM	Compagnie Generale Maritime (France)
CORFO	Production Development Corporation of Chile
CTST	Calcutta State Transport Corporation
EDF	Electricite de France
ESB	Electricity Supply Board (Ireland)
ETA	Ethiopian Telecommunications Authority
HMT	Hindustan Machine Tools (India)
IPE	Instituto dos Participacoes do Estado (Portugal)
IRI	Istituto per la Ricostinzione Industriale (Italy)
KTDA	Kenya Tea Development Authority
OR	operating ratio
PT	production target
SEST	Special Secretariat for Control of State Enterprises (Brazil)
SNCF	French State Railways
SODECI	Societe de Distribution d'Eau de la Cote d'Ivoire (Ivory Coast)
SOE	state-owned enterprise
TANESCO	Tanzanian Electric Supply Company Limited

Table of Contents

I.   Introduction...1

       The Nature of SOEs....................................2
       The Performance of SOEs..............................10

II.   Defining Objectives....................................17

       The Costs of Noneconomic Goals.......................18
       Mechanisms for Setting Objectives....................20

III.   Control Without Interference..........................21

       The Institutional Link Between Government
            and Enterprise..................................23
       The Price of Finance................................29

IV.   Holding Managers Accountable for Results.............30

       Performance Evaluation...............................30
       Information on Performance...........................38
       Pressures from Competition, Clients,
            and the Public.................................42

V.   Managerial Incentives and Skills.....................45

       Incentives Linked to Results.........................45
       SOE Managerial Skills...............................48

VI.   Liquidation...54

VII.   Divestiture...56

VIII. Alternatives to State Ownership.......................61

IX.   Agenda for Reform.....................................69

Table of Contents (Contd.)

Annex A: Contracts between the State and its Enterprises:
          The Experience of France and Senegal....................77

Annex B: The Pakistan Signaling System...........................88

Statistical Appendix..95

Bibliography..98

<u>Figures</u>

1. Growth of Nonfinancial State-owned Enterprises..................5

2. Nonfinancial State-owned Enterprises' Share of GDP..............7

3. State-owned Enterprises' Share of GDP by Sector.................8

4. State-owned Enterprises' Share of Value Added in
   Manufacturing..9

5. Net Claims of Nonfinancial State-owned Enterprises
   on the budget...14

<u>Tables</u>

1. Profits and Subsidies of SOEs in Selected Countries............11

2. Indicators of SOE Profitability, Selected Countries............12

3. Nonfinancial SOE Share in Total Domestic Credit at
   Year's End...15

4. Nonfinancial SOEs share of Nonagricultural
   Employment...18

5. The Divergence between Economic and Financial
   Profitability in Major Subsectors of Egyptian
   Public Industry, 1980-81.....................................33

6. The Sale of SOEs in Chile, 1974 to August, 1982...............57

7. The Main Alternatives to SOEs in Selected Sectors.............62

I. Introduction

State-owned enterprises (SOEs) are increasingly important actors in developing economies. They often dominate key sectors; they are significant borrowers in domestic and world credit markets; and they control the trade of major export and consumer goods. Furthermore, SOEs command a sizable and growing share of public resources in many countries. Consequently, more and more attention has been focused on whether SOEs are performing efficiently.

Theory and experience suggest that efficiency is greatest when an enterprise strives to maximize profits in a competitive market, under managers with the autonomy, motivation, and capability to respond to the challenge of competition. Inefficient enterprises would be allowed to go bankrupt and be liquidated. But SOEs seldom confront such circumstances. Rather, they are expected to achieve noncommercial goals that often conflict with profit maximization. Many face noncompetitive markets; the absence of competition is a common reason for creating SOEs. Their autonomy is often compromised by government intervention in their operating decisions. Managers may not be held accountable for results or given the incentives to perform well, and the way managers are selected, trained, and rewarded may not be appropriate for a commercial enterprise. Furthermore, nonviable SOEs are seldom liquidated.

These special constraints need not be an excuse for poor performance, as this paper attempts to show. The discussion begins by providing background information on the nature and size of the SOE sector and some performance indicators. The main part of the paper focuses on ways to create circumstances that can enhance SOE operating efficiency. These include:

- setting clear and attainable objectives linked to
  performance criteria,

- achieving control while reducing undue interference,

- holding managers accountable for results,

- designing managerial incentives and developing a cadre of
  managers with appropriate skills.

The discussion closes with a review of alternatives to state ownership and the
issues involved in liquidating and privatizing SOEs.

The Nature of SOEs

The term state-owned enterprise is used here in the broadest sense to
mean all industrial and commercial firms, mines, utilities, transport
companies, and financial intermediaries controlled to some extent by
government. SOEs are distinguished from the rest of the government because
they are expected to earn most of their revenue from the sale of goods and
services, are self-accounting, and have a separate legal identity. This
definition of state enterprise also implies the concept of an expected return
on investment. Thus, hospitals, universities, or similar institutions would
be excluded. The other characteristic of an SOE that separates it from a
government department or a private firm is the degree of public control, a
feature that is especially hard to define. In theory, a state enterprise is
less directly controlled by government than a department, given its separate
legal character. But it is still under greater government control than a
private firm. One crucial distinction is that the government appoints the
chief executive officer (CEO), or appoints the board or body that then
appoints the CEO. This usually means 50 percent or greater public ownership,
but could occur with as little as 10 percent if the other shareholders are
dispersed.

In practice, countries vary widely in what they choose to operate as
state enterprises. The telephone system is a public corporation in Jamaica,

for example, and a department in Mauritius and Bangladesh. The Indian Railways, India's largest commercial organization--indeed one of the largest in the world--is a government department that functions with more autonomy than many SOEs. This situation illustrates the problem of finding a precise definition for state enterprises.

The circumstances and characteristics of SOEs also appear to vary widely. A state enterprise might be a natural monopoly or a competitive manufacturing firm. It might be operating in a command economy surrounded by other SOEs, or it may be one of a handful of state firms in a predominantly free market. In practice, however, SOEs share many qualities. Most economies are a mixture of markets and central controls, and, whatever their mixture may be, the problems of trying to assure SOE efficiency are strikingly similar. Conflicting objectives, insufficient SOE autonomy, inadequate measures for judging performance, lack of incentives linked to performance, and bureaucratic rather than commercial management styles--these problems arise in all sectors and have prompted attempts at reform in socialist and market economies alike. When such reforms fail, the consequences are also similar. Every economy finds that financial weaknesses in SOEs affect other public and private firms. The latter suffer if SOEs command financial resources to which others might ordinarily be entitled, or if they fail to supply promised goods or services, or run up large arrears.

Increased SOE efficiency typically requires internal improvement-- better financial management, more careful inventory control, and a balanced production line, for example. But these reforms will not solve the wider problems of SOE-government relations. This report concentrates on these common problems of SOEs and suggests ways of tackling them. Of course, suggestions have to be tailored to the characteristics of individual firms and countries. A government's approach toward a manufacturing SOE selling in competitive export markets will differ from its treatment of a large, natural monopoly. The former might be required to maximize profits, whereas the latter might have its prices set according to its marginal cost, or it might be required to minimize costs. Similarly, the options of countries will vary. A large country might fire poor SOE managers and replace them with better ones; a small country might have no alternative but to try to improve the skills of its less capable managers.

The number of SOEs appears to be on the rise; Figure 1 shows the increase for a sample of eight countries. Governments cite many reasons for creating SOEs. Some see state ownership as a way to correct perceived market failures, including a small, highly risk-averse private sector. Others believe that SOEs may raise revenues, increase employment, promote regional development, redistribute income, and encourage (or discourage) a particular national group. SOEs are also perceived as a way to achieve independence from foreign companies and to direct the course of development by controlling key sectors. Some SOEs are created as a channel for development aid. As for the reasons given for embodying an activity in a public corporation rather than a government department, this arrangement is said to increase flexibility through decentralization, escape the inefficiency or corruption of central bureaucracies, attract different personnel, and apply different incentives outside the civil service pay limits.

Differences in classification and accounting make it difficult to speak about world trends in SOEs. Information on SOEs is neither collected nor consolidated in many countries, including until recently Brazil, which has over 560 SOEs. What data are available point toward an increase in the resources and employment of public companies. In developing countries for

Figure 1
Growth of nonfinancial state-owned enterprises

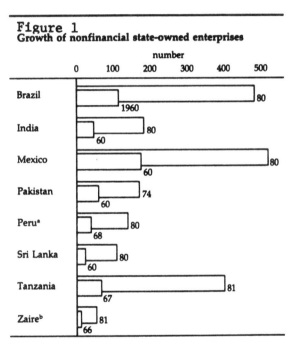

The length of the bars indicates the number of majority state-owned enterprises in selected countries for specific years. Local government SOEs are not included.

a. Includes minority shareholdings.
b. 100 percent state-owned enterprises only.

which information is available, the contribution of national, nonfinancial SOEs to value added increased from 6.8 percent in the early 1970s to about 10 percent in 1980. 1/ These figures understate the rise in SOEs because little data are available on local government SOEs. These have been growing even faster than national ones in larger countries such as Brazil and India. The SOE share of investment has also grown, from about 20 percent in the early 1970s to more than 30 percent by the late 1970s for twenty-five developing countries. 2/ The figures for some individual countries are even more striking (see Appendix Tables 1 and 2). In a few countries, SOEs also employ a sizable share of the labor force. Nonfinancial state firms employ more than 30 percent of the nonagricultural labor force in Benin, Tanzania, and Zambia (see Appendix Table 3).

This rise of SOEs in developing countries has brought their contribution to GDP to a level similar to that prevalent in many developed countries during the 1970s. 3/ As Figure 2 shows, SOEs account for about 10 percent of GDP in a striking number of countries with very different levels of per capita income. Some hypothesize that this similarity reflects the fact that governments in market economies often create SOEs to cope with common economic problems. 4/ Some support to this view is found in the similar patterns of heavy SOE involvement in utilities, transportation, and communications compared with little or no involvment in agriculture and commerce (Figure 3). Alternatively, there is little discernible pattern of ownership in mining and manufacturing (see also Figure 4). To some extent this could reflect different endowments of resources and levels of industrialization. SOEs tend to be prevalent where mining is a significant source of revenue and foreign exchange, where oil is a prominent resource, and where large-scale manufacturing is important. Although the data are sketchy,

Figure 2
Nonfinancial state-owned enterprises' share of GDP

GNP per capita (1980 dollars)

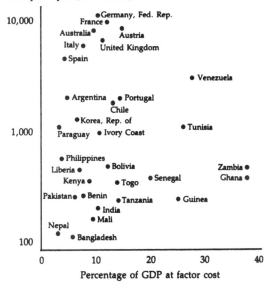

This figure shows that, for many countries with different levels of GNP per capita, SOEs' share of GDP is close to 10 percent.

Sources: UNIDO; World Bank; Peter Short (1983).

Figure 3
State-owned enterprises' share of GDP by sector

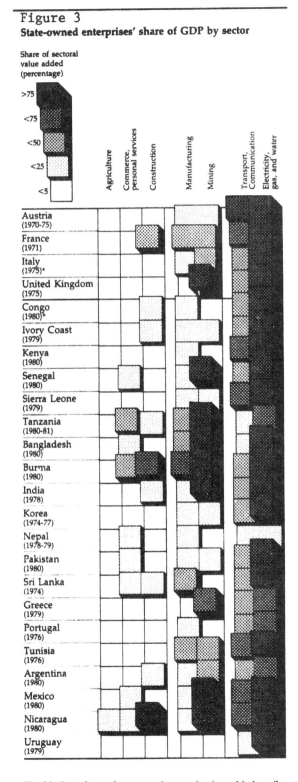

The blocks indicate the range of sectoral value added attributed to SOEs. The color and height of the blocks indicate percentage shares. Developed countries are shown first, followed by developing countries grouped by region.

a. Enterprises with more than twenty employees.
b. Gross output.

Sources: UNIDO; World Bank; Peter Short (1983).

- 9 -

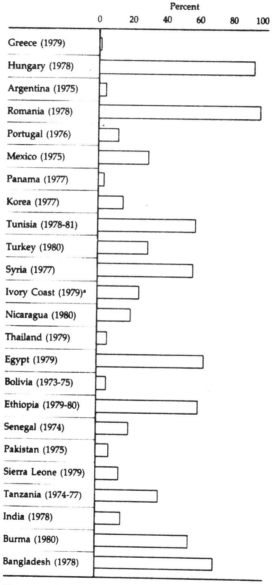

Figure 4
State-owned enterprises' share of value added in manufacturing

The twenty-four developing countries shown above are listed in descending order of 1980 GDP per capita. The length of the bars indicates the percentage of the countries' manufacturing value added attributed to nonfinancial SOEs.

a. Includes mining.

Sources: UNIDO; World Bank; Peter Short (1983).

it appears that developing countries are prone to rely on public financial intermediaries: they have been responsible for more than 75 percent of the financial sector value added in Burma, Korea, Mexico, Nicaragua, Pakistan, and Sri Lanka; 50 percent in the Congo, Senegal, and Uruguay; and between 25 and 50 percent in Argentina and Bolivia. Public ownership is far less prevalent in the financial systems of developed countries. One possible explanation for this difference is that governments in developing countries believe they lack the financial flexibility and institutions to rely on other tools, such as banking regulations and open market operations, to control the financial sector.

The Performance of SOEs

The different classifications of SOEs make it difficult to generalize about their financial performance. Moreover, the few data that are available do not allow an assessment of return to capital and provide only a general indication of results. 5/ Nonfinancial SOEs in twenty-four developing countries, for example, earned an average operating surplus before depreciation of about 1.3 percent of GDP in 1977. 6/ This estimate overstates profits, since no account was taken of interest payments, subsidized inputs, taxes, or accumulated arrears. Proper provision for these items and depreciation would put the SOEs in many of these countries in the red, as Table 1 shows. A study of sixty-four SOEs in twenty-six countries in the 1960s found that when a normal depreciation was included, and subsidies excluded, the companies showed a loss equivalent to 16 percent of total activity (operating revenues less operating expenditures). 7/ Individual country experience also indicates that return on investment is often low or negative and self-financing of investment is close to nil (see Table 2).

Table 1 Profits and Subsidies of SOEs in Selected Countries
(as a percentage of GDP at market prices)

| | After Tax Profit/Loss (-) | | Current Subsidies | Gross Margin (Surplus/Deficit Before Subsidies, Interest, and Depreciation) |
	Before Depreciation	After Depreciation a/		
Industrialized countries				
Australia (1974-77)	1.0	--	n.a.	2.2
Canada (1978-80)	1.1	0.4	n.a.	n.a.
France (1978-81) b/	1.2	n.a.	0.7	1.1
Italy (1978-80)	-0.3	-2.0	n.a.	n.a.
Japan (1978-80)	1.0	-0.1	n.a.	n.a.
Netherlands (1978)	2.3	0.6	n.a.	n.a.
Norway (1977-80)	0.8	n.a.	n.a.	n.a.
Developing countries				
Africa				
Botswana (1978-79)	1.7	0.9	n.a.	4.9
Ivory Coast (1978-79)	2.8	n.a.	n.a.	n.a.
Malawi (1978)	2.9	1.5	0.0	n.a.
Mali (1978) c/	-2.0	-3.0	n.a.	-0.9
Senegal (1974) d/	4.9 (0.0)	3.2 (-1.4)	n.a.	n.a.
Tunisia (1978-80)	3.4	0.6	n.a.	n.a.
Asia				
Burma (1978-80)	1.7	n.a.	n.a.	n.a.
India (1978)	1.7	0.4	0.6	3.6
Korea (1978-80)	2.1	n.a.	n.a.	n.a.
Thailand (1978-80)	1.2	n.a.	0.1	n.a.
Europe, Middle East				
Portugal (1978-80)	n.a.	n.a.	4.5	n.a.
Turkey (1978-80)	0.8	-0.1	2.7	-1.4
Western Hemisphere				
Argentina (1976-77)	2.1	n.a.	1.0	n.a.
Barbados (1978-80)	0.3	n.a.	1.3	n.a.
Bolivia (1974-77)	2.4	n.a.	0.1	8.0
Chile (1978-80) b/	1.5	n.a.	0.3	8.2
Colombia (1978-80)	1.0	n.a.	0.3	1.5
Dominican Republic (1978-79) b/	0.3	n.a.	0.7	n.a.
Guatemala (1978-80)	0.3	n.a.	0.0	0.5
Guyana (1978-80)	6.5	n.a.	1.1	13.5
Jamaica (1978-80) b/	1.3	n.a.	1.2	n.a.
Mexico (1978) b/	1.5	n.a.	0.9	4.9
Panama (1978-79)	0.6	-1.8	0.4	n.a.
Paraguay (1978-80)	1.4	n.a.	0.1	2.2
Peru (1978-79)	0.6	n.a.	0.1	n.a.
Uruguay (1978-80)	2.3	n.a.	0.3	3.8

Note: Gross margin is sales revenue less operating expenditures excluding
   depreciation and interest. Profits equal gross margin plus current
   transfers and subsidies less interest, dividends, and taxes. These data
   are not fully comparable because of differences in the treatment of SOE
   taxes, subsidies, and finance charges.

a/   At replacement cost for most countries. The basis of measurement for
     several African countries is unknown.

b/   Major enterprises only.

c/   Eight large enterprises only.

d/   Figures in parentheses exclude the phosphate company.

Source: P. Short, 1983.

Table 2   Indicators of SOE Profitability, Selected Countries
(percentage)

	1970	1971	1972	1973	1974	1975	1976	1977	1978	1979	1980	1981	1982
Sri Lanka:													
Net profits/ capital employed				9.4	18.0	10.5	-0.5				13.0		
Nepal:													
Gross profits/ capital employed	5.9			3.7				2.6					
India:													
Gross profits/ capital employed a/		4.1	5.1	6.2	8.4	7.6	9.4	7.5	7.7	7.6	7.8	12.2	
Net after tax profits/ capital employed a/		-4.6	2.7	1.1	2.6	0.2	1.7	-0.8	-0.3	-0.5	-1.0	2.2	
Pakistan:													
Manufacturing SOEs, net after tax profits/ fixed assets									1.0	0.6	3.4	2.8	5.7
equity									3.5	2.6	14.8	11.1	21.9
Mali:													
Net losses/sales						-0.4	-3.0	-3.5	-11.3				
Mexico:													
Investment self-financing b/	66.7	33.7	29.1	-0.1	-13.5	20.3	8.2	-10.6	-1.8	.05			
Turkey:													
Manufacturing SOEs, gross profits/sales		4.4	0.8	1.0	-4.7	-10.3	-23.2	-20.3	-16.6	-2.0			
Investment self-financing c/		28.0	30.8	16.3	-2.4	-23.7	-40.9	-41.8	-34.3	-3.2			

Note: These data are not fully comparable across countries because of
     different classifications, accounting standards, taxation, and access of
     SOEs to government current transfers and subsidized inputs.

a/   By fiscal years.
b/   Current savings (before depreciation less transfers/total investment)
c/   Net after tax profits (before depreciation)/total investment.

Source: World Bank files.

This poor aggregate performance is especially disturbing since SOEs often control some of the potentially largest revenue-earning activities, such as petroleum or mining.

Another cause of concern is that these poor financial results mean little or no self financing of investment, rising debt, and a growing burden on the treasury. In a sample of twenty-seven developing countries in 1976-79, the net budgetary burden (government subsidies, transfers, and net lending to SOEs less dividends and interest payments to government) averaged more than 3 percent of GDP. 8/ Current subsidies and other transfers alone represented 1.4 percent of GDP. (See Figure 5 for data from twelve developing countries.) The budgetary burden of SOEs in developed countries, meanwhile, averaged about 2 percent of GDP in seven countries in 1976-79. The budgetary burden includes capital transfers and lending, which is in part a desirable government equity and debt contribution to SOE investment. But in many cases a large government contribution to investment reflects the inability of enterprises to self-finance a part of their investment program. In addition, it is not unusual for SOEs to use capital infusions to finance current expenses.

Many SOE investment programs are based on a level of self-financing or debt-servicing capacity that never materializes. This failure to generate expected capital is often more troublesome than operating losses, especially where SOEs or ministries are aggressive in developing and promoting investment projects. Peru's SOEs, for example, are profitable in the aggregate. They earned a 4 percent return on equity in 1980. But ambitious investment programs and a failure, for many reasons, to generate expected returns, led some companies into growing indebtedness and reliance on government capital transfers. Peru's government is implementing programs to improve SOE

Figure 5
Net claims on the budget of nonfinancial state-owned enterprises

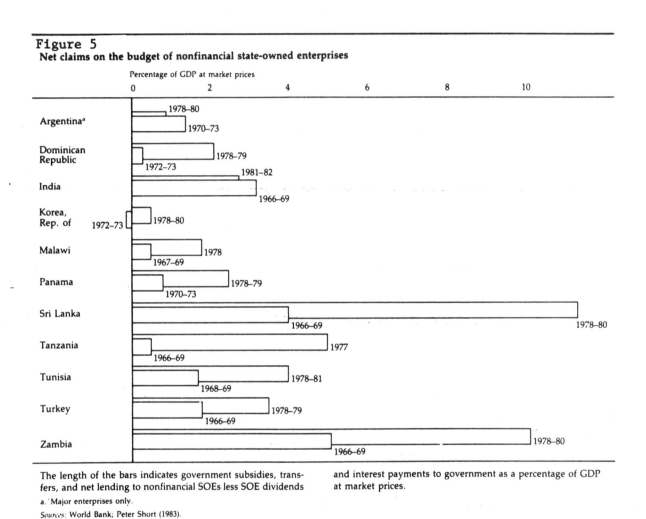

Percentage of GDP at market prices

The length of the bars indicates government subsidies, transfers, and net lending to nonfinancial SOEs less SOE dividends and interest payments to government as a percentage of GDP at market prices.

a. Major enterprises only.

Sources: World Bank; Peter Short (1983).

management, curb unreasonable demands on its enterprises, control debts, and scrutinize investments more carefully.

In addition, SOEs are important borrowers. Nonfinancial SOEs accounted for 28 percent of all Eurocurrency borrowing in 1980. 9/ They were responsible for 40 percent or more of all domestic credit outstanding in Benin, Burma, Gambia, Guinea, and Indonesia in the early 1980s (see Table 3).

Table 3   Nonfinancial SOE Share in Total Domestic Credit at Year's End
(percentage)

Indonesia	(1980)	91.5	Sudan	(19981)	22.5
Guinea	(1980)	87.1	Togo	(1979)	22.4
Burma	(1980)	76.4	Guyana	(1981)	20.7
Benin	(1980)	54.2	Ghana	(1980)	20.7
Gambia	(1981)	40.5	Yemen Arab		
Bolivia	(1977)	40.3	Republic	(1980)	18.5
Bangladesh	(1981)	39.3	Turkey	(1981)	16.5
Senegal	(1978)	38.7	Haiti	(1981)	15.6
Mali	(1978)	37.9	Pakistan	(1981)	15.0
Somalia	(1981)	37.9	Malawi	(1981)	14.7
Niger	(1980)	32.4	Egypt	(1981)	13.9
Ivory Coast	(1979)	29.0	Peru	(1981)	11.8
Upper Volta	(1978)	27.8	Mauritania	(1980)	7.9
Portugal	(1980)	24.1	Jamaica	(1981)	7.2
			Greece	(1979)	6.8

Source: Peter Short, 1983

The possible causes of low SOE profits are many. State firms typically face controlled prices that limit their return, and they are often required to undertake social welfare tasks that add to expenses. But the evidence also points to substantial room for efficiency gains in state enterprises. Underutilization of capacity, excess inventories, poor quality merchandise, frequent power outages, and late trains are well known.

Instances of inefficiency range from a South Asian public company whose huge inventory of spare parts exceeds the net worth of its equipment while most of its machines are out of service, to an African water supply company that can only account in its billings for one-half of the water it pumps, or a South American state fishing firm that borrowed millions in foreign exchange to purchase fishing boats in kits that remained unassembled seven years later. However, systematic studies measuring SOE efficiency against that of similar private firms or some sort of international norm are rare.

Comparisons of public and private firms in developed countries give conflicting evidence. 10/ Such comparisons are always difficult and are even more of a problem in developing countries. Public and private firms in developing countries usually operate in entirely different sectors or, if not, use different production mixes. The SOEs are much more capital intensive and larger in terms of labor force. The skimpy evidence that is available points to higher efficiency in private enterprises in manufacturing. For example, from 1965 to 1975 average labor productivity in Turkey's manufacturing SOEs increased by 9 percent a year in the private sector and 7 percent a year in the public sector. In 1979 average labor productivity was 30 percent higher in the private than in the public manufacturing sector. (The average public firm is about ten times the size of the average private one and about 50 percent more capital intensive.) From 1970 to 1974, labor productivity rose by 15.2 percent in Tanzania's private manufacturing firms and fell by almost 25 percent in the state-owned firms. 11/

Additionally, a study of Turkey's manufacturing firms found that while the growth in total factor productivity from 1963 to 1976 was higher in SOEs, the level was lower. In 1976, state firms required 1 percent more labor and 43.6 percent more capital per unit of output than private ones. 12/

(These estimates assume that the raw material input per unit of output was the same in public and private plants in any given industry.)

A modest improvement in efficiency could have substantial impact. For example, a 5 percent increase in SOE revenues plus a 5 percent drop in costs would generate resources amounting to:

- almost 2 percent of GDP in Turkey, or 10 percent of tax revenues

- some 1.5 percent of GDP in Tanzania, enough to finance all its spending on health

- as much as 2.2 percent of GDP in Mali--roughly two-thirds of expenditure on education or twice that on health

- some 1.4 percent of GDP in Bolivia--14 percent of tax revenue or one and a half times the spending on health.

A 5 percent increase in the turnover of Zambia's manufacturing holding company, ZIMCO, would free resources equivalent to almost 90 percent of government spending on education.

II. Defining Objectives

One of the most important and difficult tasks for governments is to clarify and rank the objectives of their SOEs. Where state enterprises are expected to pursue both commercial and social goals and to answer many different constituencies, their performance will suffer unless they are given a clear sense of priorities. Without that, their results cannot be measured against expectations, while losses can be too easily attributed to social goals and poor management thereby concealed.

The Costs of Noneconomic Goals

SOEs are frequently expected to contribute to the broader goals of government policy. The consequences can be perverse. 13/ For instance, SOE prices may be controlled to benefit the poor or assist counterinflationary policies. But SOE consumers are often large industrial users, wholesalers, or the upper and middle classes, so they—not the poor—benefit most. In Egypt, for example, almost two-thirds of energy subsidies in 1979 went to the urban areas, only about one-third to the poorer rural areas; of the subsidies to the urban population, almost 40 percent went to the richest 20 percent of the population. 14/ Furthermore, the costs of subsidies are shifted from the consumer to the taxpayer, or, if the deficit is financed through inflationary monetary expansion, to the public at large. Given the regressive nature of taxes in many developing countries and the impact of inflation of the poor, the net effect may be to increase income inequalities.

Since SOEs are often capital intensive, they can make only a limited contribution to alleviating unemployment. In a survey of twenty-three developing countries in 1979-82, nonfinancial SOEs were responsible for an average of less than 15 percent of nonagricultural employment (Table 4).

Table 4   Nonfinancial SOEs' Share of Nonagricultural Employment

	OECD Countries	Developing Countries				
		Total	Africa	Asia	Latin America	N. Africa
Average share (%)	4.1	13.9	18.7	15.7	5.5...10.3	
Number of countries	14	18	8	4	5.......1	

Source: Peter Heller and Allen Tait, "Government Employment and Pay: Some International Comparisons."   Forthcoming in the IMF Occasional Paper series.   See also Appendix Table 3.

Nevertheless, SOEs are often used to expand employment, and thus are also responsible for overstaffing, which tends to lower morale and run up excessive wage bills that can damage an SOE's financial position. Other ways of creating employment may be less costly and more productive. For example, overstaffing in Egypt's SOEs was estimated at 20 percent in 1975. If the wages of these approximately 200,000 redundant workers had been invested, they could have created an estimated 38,800 productive jobs a year (assuming an average wage of 2,500 L.E. per job). Thus, "by 1981, the original false jobs would all have been replaced and value-added ... would have increased by 11 percent, generating real resources for further employment increases." 15/

Where noncommercial achievements are expected of SOEs, a government can judge the net gain (or loss) to society only by making these goals explicit and calculating their costs and benefits. Often it is better to let an enterprise operate on commercial, profit-seeking lines and then use its profits to achieve social goals. A commercially oriented SOE can be a most effective tool for improving social welfare, as exemplified by the experience of the Kenya Tea Development Authority (KTDA). KTDA was created as a 100 percent state-owned enterprise. In roughly two decades it organized the planting of 54,000 hectares of tea by some 138,000 smallholders and became the world's largest exporter of black tea. KTDA was set up as a commercial enterprise and was not given many secondary welfare responsibilities that might have weakened its financial autonomy. Because of its commercial orientation, KTDA has been able to develop an industry that substantially benefits approximately one million members of tea growers' households, as well as laborers, traders, and others in the tea districts. 16/

Where an SOE is required to pursue noncommercial goals, the added expenses should be estimated in advance and financed through the budget. If it is not reimbursed, the SOE will be decapitalized, morale will suffer, and the quality of its goods and services will deteriorate. For example, many countries keep railway fares artificially low. The burden to the treasury can grow out of proportion; often the cost grows to the point where poorer countries cannot afford to pay all of it. The railway is then compelled to cut costs, usually by deferring maintenance and replacement investment. The result is a deterioration in service that hurts those sectors of the economy that depend most on railway transport.

Unfortunately, governments often reimburse their SOEs with an automatic, cost plus subsidy, which can erode financial discipline and reward the inefficient. Studies of railway subsidies show that rising subsidies are often associated with slower growth of labor productivity--yet wages continue to grow as fast as industrial wages in general--or with much faster increases in railway labor costs than labor costs in industry in general. 17/ The availability of subsidies can cause management to relax emphasis on cost minimization and weaken resistance to pressures for wage increases. This is always the risk with subsidies; but the risk can be minimized by specifying the SOEs' social welfare goals, carefully calculating the added expense, and monitoring agreed upon indicators of performance.

Mechanisms for Setting Objectives

In practice it is hard to define targets for SOEs by an assessment of costs and benefits. Often there are strong political motives for keeping objectives fuzzy and not analyzing the tradeoffs involved. Nevertheless, some governments have made important efforts to clarify objectives, as in France and Senegal, where they have negotiated formal contracts with SOEs to establish a clearer operating framework (see Annex A). Under such arrangements, governments pledge to meet their financial and other obligations and to eschew ad hoc interference; in exchange, SOEs accept negotiated performance targets. The experience of both these countries shows that the contract itself is less important than the process of preparing and negotiating it. The agreements help both parties to translate vague intentions into quantifiable goals. The SOE must first develop a comprehensive corporate plan and the government must assess the plan in light of its priorities and constraints. Contracts also make the costs of achieving objectives more transparent, thus allowing a more rational consideration of costs and benefits. In Senegal, for example, loss-making air services to remote areas were cut back after Air Senegal presented an estimate of losses per passenger kilometer.

The negotiations allow the parties to anticipate potential conflicts and work them out beforehand and to develop procedures for resolving future disputes. For this very reason, the time and effort required to produce and negotiate a contract can be substantial (as much as two years in both Senegal and France). Yet, the time spent can be highly beneficial, since it is essential to clarify goals and policies, and should also increase the participants' commitment to implementing the contracts. The two-way nature of negotiations also increases the SOE's willingness to comply with the contract. Notwithstanding this commitment, subsequent monitoring of results plus incentives and sanctions linked to performance is essential to success. Contracts also need to be renegotiated if they are threatened by unforeseen economic developments.

III. Control without Interference

SOE autonomy needs to be blended with some central control. Unless governments monitor the performance of their SOEs and take the main decisions

on investment and debt, their macroeconomic management will be undermined, as
Brazil's experience has demonstrated. Until 1979 the Brazilian government had
no consolidated information on earnings, spending, or debt of its more than
350 SOEs. 18/ It therefore had no way of comparing consolidated public
investment with financial resources, so public investment often exceeded the
amount of money actually available, thereby increasing inflation and the
country's foreign debt. Moreover, in addition to their own revenues earned on
the sale of goods and services, the state enterprises received substantial
transfers from the government. These included earmarked tax revenues, credits
from official financial institutions, interenterprise transfers, and loan
guarantees. With the multiplication of these extrabudgetary funds, control
over the economic and financial operations of SOEs was gradually eroded.
Projects were started without adequate provision for their financing, and
supplementary transfers were often required to prevent large-scale layoffs and
defaults to suppliers, contractors, and creditors. Furthermore, the size of
the public sector grew as SOEs invested their--often monopoly--profits in the
creation of numerous subsidiaries. The petroleum company, for example, set up
more than seventy such firms and branched into marketing, fertilizers,
export/import, and petrochemicals.

Yet, while central control is necessary, it can itself be poorly
organized. All too often, different official agencies intervene in SOE
decisions that should be the prerogative of management, and government fails
to coordinate their action. Too much interference can be combined with too
little control. In addition, policy that swings between autonomy and central
control can prevent coherent direction of SOEs. In particular, governments
tend to overreact to SOE abuses of their independence, especially in times of
financial crisis.

Here again, the example of Brazil is illustrative. Faced with
growing inflationary pressures and a deteriorating balance of payments, the
government in 1979 phased out most of the SOEs' earmarked taxes and
centralized authority over SOE finances in a new agency in the Planning
Ministry, the Special Secretariat for Control of State Enterprises (SEST).
SEST is responsible for approving and monitoring the budgets for 382 SOEs and
autonomous institutions. These are summarized in an annual SEST budget
authorized by the president. All foreign and domestic credit operations by an
SOE require prior SEST approval, as do any proposals to create, expand, or
liquidate any state enterprise.

SEST also places entity-by-entity limits on imports and fuel
consumption and intervenes in salary and pension decisions. So far, the
Planning Ministry and SEST have been primarily concerned with setting and
enforcing firm-by-firm ceilings. They have not become seriously involved in
evaluating SOE investment plans, but this may change as a result of the first
multiyear consolidation of government investment programs in 1982.

Consolidated information and central control of SOE debt and
investment was long overdue in Brazil. The intervention in import and fuel
purchases and salaries and benefits, however, could mark a worrisome trend
toward excessive centralization. The controls were introduced in response to
a financial crisis, and it is too early to judge how SEST will operate in more
normal times. The challenge is to design a system that holds management
accountable for results while giving it the autonomy to achieve them.

The Institutional Link between Government and Enterprise

In an effort to reduce arbitrary intervention by the government,
countries have devised institutional arrangements that place the government at
arm's length from the SOE. Boards of directors or holding companies have been

widely used to create a buffer between SOE management and the central bureaucracy, to provide policy direction, and to report on results. Special bureaus, commissions, and ministries have become a popular way of centralizing information and control of SOEs.

Administrative reforms often begin and end with changes to the institutional arrangements. These arrangements have a mixed record, however, showing that institutional changes alone rarely achieve a satisfactory balance between independence and control. Furthermore, arrangements that work well for one country or enterprise may not do so elsewhere. For example, the Ethiopian Telecommunications Authority (ETA) functioned relatively well with a politically oriented board of directors dominated by a minister—an arrangement that has proved disastrous in other countries.

ETA's board has not interfered in the daily operations of the company. The general manager is recruited from the ranks and is expected to run the company as a commercial operation within the guidelines set by the board. ETA's board has powers usually split among several ministries and agencies. It sets tariffs, hires and fires the manager, and approves ETA's staffing plan, budget, and investments. The general manager, in turn, is also powerful and can fire incompetent staff, compete in the domestic capital market, and make the necessary decisions to implement the company's plans.

By contrast, the boards of directors of SOEs in Turkey act as conduits for direct government control of all facets of operations. The boards are made up of the director general; directors representing the Ministry of Finance, the SOE's oversight ministry, and the labor unions; and two assistant directors. The oversight ministry appoints the director general and assistant directors and runs the day-to-day operations of the company through the board, which sits in permanent session. Managers are virtually civil servants, and the SOEs were, until recently, run more like government departments than independent concerns.

The experience with SOE boards in most developing countries lies somewhere between these two examples, closer to that of Peru. There, the members are part-time; many have full-time civil service jobs in the oversight ministries. Typically, they have little business experience and are changed frequently. Such boards do little to guide the SOE. Instead, the company's executive director must spend a lot of time educating new, inexperienced board members and overcoming tendencies toward risk aversion and inertia. On the positive side, the boards are a source of early information on the firm and occasionally win support for its decisions from the ministries and the public.

To avoid such direct control, many countries rely on holding companies, some of which have proved to be a useful way of achieving government aims while giving SOEs greater discretion in day-to-day operational matters. Others have become counterproductive, substituting one form of ex-ante bureaucratic intervention for another. An added drawback of introducing an extra layer of bureaucracy is that it uses more scarce managerial resources.

The Istituto per la Ricostinzione Industriale (IRI) in Italy has been credited with cooperating with government to achieve its social goals while freeing the individual enterprises to pursue profits. Nevertheless, IRI, too, has been caught between conflicting government aims--such as the directive to make profits and yet support failing subsidiaries to bolster employment. From 1933, when it was created, until the mid-1960s IRI operated under the principal of nonintervention; Italy's manufacturing SOEs were allowed to operate very much like private companies. Managers of individual companies were instructed to pursue profits in a competitive environment; investments were made to promote new sectors; and, particularly during the postwar reorganization, firms were merged and liquidated. 19/

By the 1970s, however, IRI's principal tasks had become the rescue of ailing industries and the development of the south of Italy, the Messogiorno. Trade union influence over the firms grew and it became virtually impossible to fire workers or liquidate companies. Prices of some items, notably telephone service, were kept below cost to serve social goals. Investment decisions were distorted by the stress on the south. Some 60 percent of total investment and 80 percent of new investment had to go to the Messogiorno. Thus, in order to be able to invest in ailing firms in the north, highly capital intensive (and occasionally nonviable) investments were made in the south.

For all these reasons, the losses of IRI's subsidiaries increased and endowment funds were set up to compensate companies for the additional costs imposed on them by the state under the so-called Doctrine of Improper Burdens. Since this doctrine was seldom translated into a clear, quantitative assessment of specific burdens, however, SOE losses were often funded regardless of the cause. This eroded financial discipline and motivated managers to concentrate more on gaining access to endowment funds through political channels than on improving the enterprises' competitive efficiency. IRI's experience shows how little even a very successful holding company can do to preserve its independence if government policy works against it.

The experience with holding companies elsewhere is similarly mixed. Pakistan, for example, created a Board of Industrial Management (BIM) in 1973 to direct twelve corporations (with about fifty production units) on the model of Italy's IRI. The BIM answered to the Ministry of Production. This four-tier hierarchy was expected to increase the autonomy of the production units. Instead, a government commission found in 1978 that it had "resulted in the gradual centralization of authority and decisionmaking at powerful points in upper tiers." 20/ Furthermore, the overlapping functions of the ministry, the BIM, and the corporations slowed decisionmaking and contributed to a "breakdown of communications between management and the enterprises and upper tiers, which lack proper understanding of the problems at the unit level." On the commission's recommendation the BIM was abolished in 1978.

A different approach to decentralizing has been tried in several Eastern European countries (Bulgaria, East Germany, Poland, and Romania), where a new administrative level has been put between the ministry and the enterprise. Here again, experience shows that structural changes by themselves are not enough to alter the underlying balance of power. Such a change was instituted in Romania, for example, when some 200 centrale, or centrals, were established there in the fall of 1969. 21/ These were large units, averaging some 8,000 employees. As originally envisioned, the centrals were to assume some of the microeconomic planning functions and most of the operational prerogatives of the ministries. In practice, however, the existing rules and laws were not altered to give the centrals the necessary power. The ministries continued to intervene directly in the enterprises and in the day-to-day operations of the centrals.

Some countries have centralized control over their SOEs in government bureaus or specialized ministries. One of the oldest of these in a developing country is India's Bureau of Public Enterprises (BPE), set up as part of the Ministry of Finance in 1965. The BPE gathers information on about 200 of India's SOEs, reviews their performance, gives technical assistance to their managers, appraises investment proposals, gives training and assists in developing training programs, helps recruit and select managers, and sets guidelines for wage agreements and standards for various aspects of production. These are broad responsibilities--especially since BPE had less than ninety professional staff in 1982.

The bureau has little power over the SOEs; rather, the government controls its enterprises through its representatives on their boards, the Finance Ministry's budgetary control, the Planning Commission's review of investment. Moreover, the frequent changes in the head of the bureau has weakened its influence. Nevertheless, its guidelines are taken seriously, especially by smaller firms.

The BPE performs a valuable function in gathering and systematizing information on the performance of SOEs. 22/ It recently developed performance targets for the next two years with the chief executive officers of the enterprises, in collaboration with the sectoral ministries. These include a target volume of production and return on capital. Each SOE has drawn up a two-year action plan on how to achieve its targets. The benchmark indicators are then used by the SOE manager and the ministry in assessing results. 23/ In 1979 the Bureau also instituted an "early warning" system, which provides quarterly data on financial performance, physical performance, and progress on investment projects. The aim is to flag problems or slippages to management and government and allow prompt remedial action.

BPE's efforts to set guidelines and standards for performance have been less successful. Some of these standards are in areas--such as wage negotiations or travel allowances--that SOE managers regard as their prerogative. The bureau has also become involved in details, for example, setting standards for factory perimeter fencing. The effort to standardize the activities of so many diverse SOEs has damaged BPE's credibility with some managers, who believe the bureau would be more helpful if it concentrated on key issues, such as technical assistance and training or facilitating SOE interactions with the government.

Boards of directors, holding companies, and central bodies can play a vital role in monitoring performance or they can become a bureaucratic bottleneck. Their role depends largely on whether a government is merely preoccupied with short-term goals, such as implementing austerity programs or curbing abuses, or also takes a broader, longer term view of the role of SOEs in the economy. The creation of these bodies has the most beneficial impact when accompanied by some of the other reforms described below.

The Price of Finance

Typically, SOEs have access to funds at low or zero cost; they can borrow with a government guarantee, which reduces their risk premium; and they are given privileged access to domestic credit. As a result, SOEs can command a substantial share of domestic resources. Budgetary transfers to Brazilian SOEs (through earmarked revenues) totaled 50 percent of government tax revenues in 1980. SOEs' foreign debts assumed by the government of Peru during 1976 to 1980 were 31 percent of the total public foreign debt in 1980. SOEs dominated domestic credit in Indonesia, Guinea, Burma, and Benin in 1980 and represent a sizable part of the share of credit in many other countries (see Table 3).

Underpricing capital, providing government guarantees, and giving SOEs privileged access to funds contributes to the misallocation of resources, the selection of excessively large-scale capital intensive projects, growing SOE indebtedness, the crowding out of private borrowers in local credit markets, and a general tendency to expand the scope of public operations. The solution is to require SOEs to pay for the opportunity cost of their capital. This would not preclude government equity investment, but it would mean an end to loans at subsidized rates, costless transfers of treasury funds (except in payment for specified noncommercial services), automatic rollover of SOE debt, and automatic access to loans from state banks.

Requiring SOEs to pay for their capital raises again the problem of clarifying and costing goals. If the government imposes a cost on its firms it should reimburse them. This philosophy is inherent in France's contracts or Italy's Doctrine of Improper Burdens. Similarly, if the SOE makes investments in accord with national priorities and its mandated goals, it should be able to command a reasonable level of equity funds. Money provided over and above these amounts should carry interest and amortization charges.

IV. Holding Managers Accountable for Results

Performance Evaluation

There are strong arguments for creating conditions in which SOEs can be instructed to maximize profits and then be judged by that standard. Profit is a composite indicator that applies positive weights (prices) to benefits (outputs) and negative weights to costs (inputs). If the prices are correct, a profit-maximizing firm strives to achieve maximum benefits for minimum costs--the definition of efficiency. For SOEs, this criterion needs modifying for four reasons: many SOEs are monopolies; the profit that is relevant for society is different from private profits; many SOE objectives conflict with profit maximization; and market prices may be distorted. These qualifications need not negate the use of profits as a guide to performance.

Monopoly. The best way to end monopoly power is to introduce competition and allow market pricing. Where that is not possible, the prices of a monopoly SOE can be set according to its marginal costs; the SOE can then be instructed to maximize profits. Although adjusting administered prices typically involves practical and political problems, the long-run benefits can be substantial. Removing price distortions helps correct the misallocation of resources and discourages waste. Nevertheless, it may be impractical to introduce marginal cost pricing or it may produce unacceptably high prices. In that case the enterprise can still be required to minimize costs. Minimum cost indicators can be developed based on international comparisons and the SOEs own previous performance.

Accounting for public profits. Some items (such as interest payments or taxes) can be excluded from public profits so as not to encourage SOE managers to waste time on activities which may be deemed irrelevant to their jobs. By excluding these items, public managers are not judged on whether they minimize taxes or engage in interest arbitrage, for example. Judging managers soley on the basis of profit, may lead to the neglect of activities, such as maintenance, which reduce profits in the short run but have a long-run benefit. Additional targets can also be set for activities such as investment, maintenance, and research, which might not be compatible with short-run profit maximization or cost minimization.

Conflicting goals. If the SOE is required to perform noncommercial roles that reduce its profits (such as hiring extra staff to increase employment or setting up a plant in a particular area to promote regional development), the government can reimburse it for the extra costs or reduce its profit target accordingly. Careful calculation is needed of the cost of noncommercial goals: if the subsidy is too high, it reduces the incentive for the company to improve its efficiency.

Distorted prices. These can be rectified by using shadow prices for assessing SOE results. Shadow prices are calculated to reflect the opportunity costs of an enterprise's inputs and outputs. For example, the price of imported fuel may be held down by a government subsidy, but SOE accounting should value it according to its world price to ensure it is used efficiently.

The results derived from shadow-price accounting can differ widely from conventional profits and losses, as one study of industrial SOEs in Egypt has demonstrated. 24/ In almost all of the twenty-seven industries sampled, the financial rate of return calculated on the basis of extensively controlled market prices pointed in opposite directions from the economic rates of return based on shadow prices (see Table 5). For example, industries producing oils, soaps, and detergents showed a 14.4 percent economic rate of return, yet financial profitability was negative; nonferrous metals earned a 15.5 percent financial rate of return, but the economic return was negative. Not only would it be misleading to judge an SOE on the basis of its financial performance, but a manager reacting to financial signals under these circumstances would make the wrong economic decision.

While these four refinements have been extensively analyzed in theoretical work, their application has proved practically and politically difficult. For example, shadow prices involve complicated calculations and are difficult to administer. Controversies can arise over any of the accounting ratios and it may prove impossible to judge a powerful SOE manager on the basis of such a debatable measure. The best solution is to move to market pricing and remove distortions wherever it is feasible, so that market prices accurately reflect the economic prices. Such an effort cannot be piecemeal, since what matters for efficiency is not the absolute level of prices but their relationship to one another; moving only one set of prices may not help matters. For example, raising the price of energy to world

Table 5: **The Divergence between Economic and Financial Profit-ability in Major Subsectors of Egyptian Public Industry, 1980/81** (percent)

	Economic Rate of Return	Financial Rate of Return
Cotton textiles	13.6	5.9
Wool textiles	5.2	11.3
Jute products	−20.8	12.1
Carpets	3.0	13.4
Oils, soaps, and detergents	14.4	−6.6
Sugar	34.2	7.1
Processed vegetables	12.3	2.2
Oils and essences	78.1	17.6
Starch and yeats	106.4	−18.6
Artificial fibers	−9.5	1.9
Nonedible oils	−11.1	3.8
Coke	−17.4	−20.7
Leather and tanning	8.3	4.1
Iron and steel	2.7	10.9
Aluminium	−21.0	12.5
Nonferrous metals	−3.1	15.5
Steel pipes	−2.0	18.9
Formed and shaped steel	6.4	11.7
Ferrous castings	−46.2	−6.7
Road motor vehicles	−32.7	−13.4
Railway carriages	16.3	12.1
Bicycles and motorcycles	−3.2	1.5
Electrical machinery	52.6	24.4
Nonelectric durables	−3.6	20.5
Ceramics	−12.8	2.4
China and glass	−16.4	20.6

Source: Bank staff calculations

levels but keeping agricultural prices artificially low may discourage productive investment in agriculture. Furthermore, there are likely to be short-run welfare and political costs that will make it difficult to remove price distortions, even though the long-run efficiency gains will probably be substantially greater.

Market pricing must go hand in hand with curbs on SOE monopoly power. Turkey gave pricing freedom to a number of its state industrial firms in 1980. As a result, the five largest manufacturing firms earned about a $6 million profit instead of an expected $11 million loss in 1981. Since many of the companies are monopolies or quasimonopolies, however, this pricing freedom creates no pressure to control costs. Rather, it provides opportunities for SOEs to overcharge their consumers, a practice that could have adverse economic consequences. For example, efficient competitive downstream industries might be bankrupted by having to pay excessive prices.

Where price controls are in effect, either the prices must be set to allow the SOE a reasonable chance of achieving its target, or the target must take price inflexibility into account. The experience of the United Kingdom illustrates the futility of trying to hold SOEs to financial targets when prices are being kept down for stabilization purposes. British SOEs are required by their statutes to break even after interest and other appropriate revenue charges, but a 1961 White Paper called for more precise goals. 25/ To meet the statutory requirement, the White Paper stipulated that SOEs should be required at least to balance their accounts over a five-year period (after interest and depreciation). In addition, each enterprise should be held to a specific target, such as the rate of return on capital employed or a level of self financing of investment. Following the White Paper, five of the nine largest nationalized industries were given target returns on net assets; four others were given revenue targets. The targets were for a four- to five-year period and were based on the past performance and actual circumstances of each company. British Rail, for example, was expected to reduce its deficit and break even as soon as possible.

During the 1960s, seven of the companies with targets came close to meeting or exceeded their goals; but in the early 1970s most fell short because of price controls and the financial targets were abandoned. Although the government in a 1967 White Paper accepted the principal that prices should be set to reflect long-run marginal costs, a preoccupation with controlling inflation during the 1970s led the authorities to curtail price increases drastically. On occasion the companies were partly compensated for price controls, but only to offset deficits. Largely as a consequence, the average pretax rate of return on capital employed (excluding subsidies) in the nationalized industries fell from 0 in 1970 to -2 percent in 1979. 26/ Targets were reintroduced following a 1978 White Paper. Although it is too early to judge SOE performance against these medium-term targets, the recession and rising wage costs have made them difficult to meet.

One system to overcome some of the practical difficulties in using profits to evaluate performance is being implemented in Pakistan (see Annex 2). The Pakistan "signaling system" uses "public profitability" in constant terms as an indicator of performance. "Public profits" are private profits adjusted for those elements that are not deemed relevant for an SOE. For example, taxes and interest, which are public benefits, are excluded so as not to encourage SOE managers to devote time to minimizing taxes or to interest arbitrage. The costs of noncommercial objectives that might affect profits (such as the extra cost of purchasing from local suppliers to encourage domestic industry) are deducted before profits are calculated and treated as an "in-kind" dividend to the government.

Since many prices are administered and since SOE managers generally cannot affect prices, it would be unfair to reward or penalize them for the effects of changing prices on profitability. Because the administration of shadow prices is a complex and controversial task, Pakistan is judging its SOE managers, for control purposes only, by trends in public profit at constant prices. This is equivalent to constructing a quantum index of profits on the basis of quantum indices of inputs and outputs. This is an acceptable approximation of efficiency in performance evaluation (though not in project evaluation), since it is concerned, at least initially, with the trend rather than the level of performance. Enterprises will be judged on the basis of their return to fixed operating assets, or public profitability, in constant terms. The performance of any individual firm will be compared with its own record over the past five years. By not comparing enterprises with one another, the system makes allowance for the fact that some enterprises operate under greater handicaps than others.

Since public profitability could encourage managers to ignore activities with current costs but future benefits (such as planning, maintenance, training, or innovation), the government and the SOEs will negotiate extra targets for these areas, assigning them weights that vary over time and from one company to another. A firm will first have to show that it can use existing resources efficiently; hence, 90 percent of its initial target may be assigned to public profitability.

At the end of the year each SOE's performance will be rated according to how close it came to meeting its composite target. The monitoring and evaluation will be done by the Experts Advisory Cell, a semiautonomous agency responsible to the Ministry of Production but financed by a levy on the SOEs themselves. The cell has been able to maintain a remarkable degree of independence and, because it is outside the government pay limitations, to attract a specialist staff. At a review meeting with the cell, managers will be able to present an explanation of their results. Good performance will be rewarded with increased autonomy and possibly with a salary bonus.

The signaling system is expected to notify managers about what the state expects of them and motivate them to comply. Two other reforms also underway in Pakistan are critical to its success--greater autonomy for SOEs and improvements in the selection and training of managers. These should create managers with the appropriate skills and give them the necessary freedom to achieve their targets. The signals the system sends government are as important as those it sends managers. If it functions properly, the system should alert the ministry when its demands are unreasonable and when the environment makes it impossible for the SOE to meet its goals. Ideally, this should lead to policy and other macroreforms to complement the internal improvements in the firms.

One strength--and weakness--of Pakistan's signaling system is its reliance on a simple, composite indicator. This reduces the difficulties in administering the system and avoids the problem of weighting diverse and often unrelated or conflicting targets. The experience of Romania, shows the problems of trying to use multiple indicators. Frequently used indicators include gross (more recently net) output, productivity measures, gross profit, capacity utilization, exports, sales, product mix, material use coefficients, and many more. 27/ The system has been criticized for being too complex in view of its overlapping, as well as potentially inconsistent, indicators, which require managerial decisions about tradeoffs. Romania is attempting to reduce the number of "success indicators" used to assess enterprise performance.

While public profitability is less ambiguous than multiple targets, it is also incomplete. Because it is based on trends, it does not indicate how close to, or far from, maximum efficiency an enterprise is operating. Moreover, it does not give government any indication of SOE performance in meeting its social goals. This could cause managers to ignore the very reason for which they were created. For example, one principal goal of manufacturing SOEs in Tanzania was to generate employment by using labor-intensive production practices. However, a study of the textile industry found that although less capital-intensive technology was often the least costly and most profitable investment, the decisionmaking process and the managerial incentive system resulted in capital-intensive investment. Managers were rewarded for implementing large projects quickly, not for spending time to develop labor intensive processes. 28/

However, systems which use more comprehensive indicators are theoretically appealing, but operationally impractical. Pakistan's signaling system seems best designed to turn around the short-run operating performance of SOEs by establishing an unambiguous and easily understood indicator of results. Once the monitoring and incentive systems are functioning, other refinements can be introduced.

Information on Performance

Assessing SOE performance requires a regular flow of reliable information. But in many developing countries the internal management information systems of SOEs are deficient or nonexistent. SOEs (as well as private companies) are not audited according to uniform standards; more than seventy developing countries have no accounting standards. Trained accountants are scarce, because in many developing countries (outside Latin America) accounting did not become part of the university curricula until after 1960. Even now there are often no uniform standards of training. Under these circumstances, neither management nor government can judge results or budget for the future.

These weaknesses are gradually being rectified. Many francophone West African countries have tried to adapt France's accounting model to their needs. This program--the OCAM plan comptable, started almost twenty years ago--has met with mixed success, partly because its application has been too inflexible, with too much reliance on expatriate experts and too little attention paid to local accounting capabilities.

The OCAM system generates information that can be used for macroeconomic analysis. This information can also be reallocated to produce cost accounts for individual enterprises. Reallocation, however, requires skilled managers and accountants to define the enterprise's needs and develop an accounting subsystem. Since the accounts must be changed on an entry-by-entry basis, the reallocation can be time-consuming if done manually. SOEs in many developing countries lack the personnel and the hardware to make these adjustments. A 1982 survey of SOEs in Madagascar, for example, found that very few had developed effective cost accounting. 29/

In Senegal, the accountancy profession has proposed a two-tiered system, in which annual external audits conforming to internationally accepted procedures would be required for all companies above a certain size and "limited review audits" would be required for all other companies. The latter would be stricter than the current standard but less comprehensive (and cheaper) than full-scale audits.

The development of uniform and credible accounting requires a trained body of practitioners as well as a system to set and review standards and to qualify accountants. To build up such a system governments need to designate an agency to be responsible for the development of accounting, establish accounting standards backed by an appropriate legal framework, assess staff needs and designate training for bookkeepers and accountants, and foster a professional association that could assume responsibility for enforcing standards. In Madagascar the government in 1979 created a state enterprise, RINDRA, to conduct administrative, financial, and performance audits of SOEs. To date RINDRA has concentrated on financial audits, which it conducts at the request of the government or the enterprise. The quality of its audits is considered good and it has been helpful in developing accounts for the smaller public companies.

SOEs must, in addition, be required to adhere to fixed standards. Heretofore, even in countries where there are high standards of accountancy in the private sector, public accounts are filled with anomalies. In Peru, for example, one SOE was found to have depreciated its plant and equipment at only 3 percent a year. Another was allowed to deduct from its operating revenues money allocated to an investment fund that caused it to show a loss instead of a profit.

Another serious problem for public and private firms alike in some countries is the lack of full inflation accounting. Developed countries have only recently begun to adjust accounts for inflation, but some inflation-prone countries, especially in Latin America, have made inflation adjustments for years. Usually, however, this is limited to a revaluation of fixed assets and not a full adjustment of the profit-and-loss statement. The effects of such an adjustment can be considerable, even when inflation is low in comparison with that in countries like Argentina or Brazil. For example, when 1982 sales are adjusted for the change in the consumer price index for 517 of the large corporations in the United States, the average annual growth rate in sales, profits, and dividends falls sharply: 30/

	Sales	Profits	Dividends
Reported	10%	6%	10%
In constant dollars	0%	2%	-1%

The combination of poor accounts, high inflation, and distorted market prices so common in developing countries can make it very difficult to judge SOE performance.

Formal accountancy procedures are not the only way by which managers can improve the information on which they base their actions. Improvements can also be obtained through a management audit, which requires the firm to establish and adhere to a basic information system and routine control procedures and to develop targets of efficiency and effectiveness. As with a financial audit, an outside auditor would check that these procedures function properly and generate reliable data that management and government can compare with targets. Many large accounting firms can now assist enterprises in setting up and using management auditing systems.

A somewhat similar management tool is the action plan, designed to focus efforts on improving efficiency and monitor the results. The experience of the Bolivian railways illustrates how action plans work in practice. The railway had three action plans between 1973 and 1979, with objectives that

ranged from reorganizing workshops and repairing rolling stock to tract
rehabilitation and maintenance. Monitored targets included the average
percentage of total cars and locomotives in operating condition during the
year, the number of staff, the turnaround time for maintenance, and the amount
of tract to be rehabilitated. Action plans specify which measures will be
taken to achieve the targets (such as training or allocation of foreign
exchange for the purchase of spare parts) and when.

Once accurate accounts are assembled, they need to be consolidated to
give the central government an overall picture of performance and of the
claims on its resources. Whereas some countries do this as a matter of
course--the Indian BPE springs to mind--others have had little or no
consolidated data. Even then, performance is hard to assess because of
numerous hidden subsidies and cross subsidies. For example, some state
enterprises in Malaysia pay little or nothing for their land, which they then
use as their equity investment in commercial projects. Because of this hidden
subsidy, their returns are overstated. 31/ In Peru the State Marketing Board
must pay 40 percent above the market price for urea from a government plant. The
board's returns are thus understated by the amount of the cross-subsidy. 32/

Pressures from Competition, Clients, and the Public

Exposing SOEs to competition can be a simple and effective way to
promote their efficiency. And if managers are required to pursue
noncommercial goals for political or social reasons, competition will help to
quantify the costs of those goals. For example, Peru recently reduced tariffs
and eliminated import quotas to force industries to compete with imports.
Some SOEs are adapting to competition, but others are severely hampered by
excess manpower and government-imposed activities or constraints. Other
firms, such as a tractor assembly plant or a steel mill, can probably only

survive behind high protective tariffs. Still others will require new capital injections if they are to compete. In all these cases, competition has increased the pressure for better performance and helped clarify the costs of keeping inefficient producers alive and of meeting noncommercial goals.

Another way to encourage competition is to split large public monopolies into smaller competing units, especially if the monopoly did not benefit from economies of scale. In Hungary, for example, at least 130 new firms were established since 1980 by breaking up horizontal trusts and large state companies. How a company responds to competition will provide a standard by which to judge performance. "Beginning in 1983 the failure of an unprofitable enterprise to improve efficiency will trigger an automatic sequence of adjustment measures, including an obligation to change the structure of production to improve management, and to release manpower." 33/

SOEs can also be encouraged to compete in export markets. Hindustan Machine Tools (HMT), for example, is a successful Indian SOE. Only about 8 percent of HMT's total sales are exported (versus a target of 20-percent), but a case study of the company found that even this limited exposure to competition contributed to HMT's dynamism and professionalism. 34/ Competition also increased HMT's access to technological and managerial innovations.

For competition to be effective in promoting efficiency, managers must be given discretion to respond to competitive pressures, which may mean reducing staff or ending unprofitable services; moreover, these measures must be accompanied by pricing freedom. Privileged SOE access to subsidized credit and inputs should also be ended; otherwise there might be a strong bias toward capital-intensive investment.

Governments cannot always arrange for their SOEs to compete. Since one reason for establishing public firms is market failure, many state firms are monopolies producing goods and services that are not traded internationally or that the government prefers to produce domestically for reasons of national security or public interest. Often, the economy may be too small to support another domestic producer.

Organized public pressure is another way of encouraging SOE efficiency even where competition is absent. Britain, for example, has consumer councils for monopolies that deal directly with domestic consumers. Although they have no executive powers, they monitor the service provided by public monopolies and act as a proxy for market forces. The Electricity Consumer Council examines not just tariffs but also power cuts, delays in connection or repairs, and responsiveness of staff to customer inquiries and complaints. To date their success has been limited:

> There is no doubt that consumer representatives have
> exerted a humanizing influence at the periphery of the
> industries and thus eased the plight of specially
> disadvantaged consumers. They have found it more
> difficult to make an impact on the mainstream of the
> business. In part, one suspects that this is because the
> government has feared that they may become additional
> lobbyists for more government subsidy and has thus denied
> them serious political support. 35/

If consumer councils can be brought to focus on all overall service rather than just on tariffs, they can pressure for better performance. Moreover, during wage negotiations they can impress on management and unions that there are three, not two, parties to industrial agreements. For councils to be effective, the industry must be required to set specific consumer performance targets related to the availability, quality, timeliness, convenience, reliability, safety, and price of the service and to publish performance indicators. Clearly there is a risk that consumers will use their councils to pressure for subsidized services and delays in justified tariff increases. The councils must be educated to the workings of the industry and be able to differentiate between price increases stemming from rising real costs and those resulting from inefficient management or wrong policy decisions.

Clients can also induce efficiency; accountability to growers was an important factor in the success of the Kenya Tea Development Authority. Tea growers sit on district tea committees and are represented on KTDA's board. Some are also shareholders in KTDA factories or on factory boards. The growers play a key role since they have strong personal incentives to hold the authority to high performance standards.

V. Managerial Incentives and Skills

Institutional success is often attributed to the presence of "a good manager." Competent staff are no doubt essential for any efficient enterprise. But they do not operate in a vacuum. They need incentives to attract and motivate them, and the power to be effective.

Incentives Linked to Results

Some of the most effective rewards are nonpecuniary—recognition, greater responsibility, promotion, and national honors. Autonomy can also be a strong incentive for SOE managers. For example, the threat of losing its independence motivated the management of the Kenya Tea Development Authority. By the same token, managers need to know that they face penalties, such as losing their jobs, for poor performance.

As for pecuniary incentives, these again raise the conundrum of how to evaluate performance. Profitability is an unreliable indicator of managerial performance when there are distorted prices, subsidies, or monopoly rents. Furthermore, SOE managers may lack the autonomy to affect profits by, for example, chosing a foreign rather than a domestic supplier or firing excess staff. Using other targets to evaluate results raises a new set of problems, as the experience of the USSR with physical indicators makes clear. Even a relatively sophisticated targeting system, such as that introduced in Burma in the mid-1970s, cannot avoid some of these difficulties. 36/ The Burmese bonus system was implemented as part of a general reform under the "Guidelines for Operating State Economic Enterprises Along Commercial Lines." Bonuses are based on the SOE's achievement of a production target (PT) and an operating ratio (OR). Although the production target is initially set in physical terms, unlike the usual socialist target, it is translated into money terms at a price fixed at the beginning of the year and can be achieved by any production mix. The operating ratio is defined as operating expenses over operating revenues, also at fixed prices. Both targets are set during the budgetary process, although there is provision for one revision. The two ratios are interdependent and mutually reinforcing; it is difficult to achieve the OR without fulfilling the PT. There is no penalty for overfulfilling the PT and an extra bonus for exceeding the OR, which is a further incentive to increase production.

The system has been credited with motivating improvements in SOE output and productivity. One SOE, for instance, introduced a new management system, reduced its permanent staff by 10,000 workers (through attrition), and undertook other improvements to achieve one of the highest bonus rates. Difficulties remain, however, including the obvious problem of setting targets under a scheme that provides an incentive for managers to underestimate capacity. The bonuses are proportionately higher for lower salary levels, a system that limits the incentive to managers. Moreover, annual targets such as the PT and OR provide no incentive for long-run efficiency, and instead may lead to neglect of maintenance and replacement of capital. There has also been some running up of inventories, since the targets can be fulfilled by producing for stock just as for sale (unless there are finance charges if the firm must borrow working capital). Further, although there have been considerable increases in SOE autonomy, the scope for improving efficiency through managerial innovations is still quite limited. In addition, since the bonus cannot exceed 50 percent of the net current surplus, the system penalizes the most profitable, and thus perhaps the most efficient.

Finally, the ultimate results from a system that rests on administered prices will depend on how accurately these prices reflect relative economic scarcities. If the prices are wrong, the system may inadvertently reward the inefficient and penalize the efficient. Thus, as with Pakistan's signaling system, in Burma the PT and OR signal the trend in an enterprise's performance but not its efficiency in relation to that of other SOEs.

Few countries have developed bonus systems that are aimed principally at top management. Rather, incentive schemes based on enterprise performance usually reward the entire labor force even though it makes more sense to award worker bonuses on the basis of individual or team performance. One drawback to linking managerial and worker rewards is the tendency to give proportionally more to workers and to reduce the incentive to management. In 1969 the Hungarian bonus system had to be changed because unions protested that managers were benefiting disproportionately in comparison with workers. "In recent years changes generally have sought to increase income differentials to stimulate productivity." 37/ Another impediment arises if the bonus becomes part of the salary structure. Prior to 1967, bonuses and premiums based on fulfillment of plan targets in Romania averaged about 20 percent of income for workers and managers. Because the entire industrial labor force participated and the payments were such a sizable part of income, it was regarded as politically impossible to avoid payment, even when the targets went unfulfilled. 38/

The proposed bonus system for Pakistan would assess managerial performance on the basis of how well the SOE met its targets, after taking into account any aspects or circumstances beyond the manager's control. The system under consideration would rank performances from A to D and award a bonus based on salary according to the ranking.

SOE Managerial Skills

The skills of a public enterprise manager need to be closer to those of his private sector counterpart than to those of a government bureaucrat. Nevertheless, in many developing countries managers are part of the civil service, or at least subject to its pay scale. Even where this is not the case, their pay seldom matches private salaries. Although the prestige and challenge of running what are often the largest corporations in the country may sometimes compensate for lower pay, low salaries tend to deter skilled managers and increase the rate of staff turnover. To give one of many examples, salaries in a public utility in Turkey averaged one-third those of the private sector in 1981, and the company has had seven general managers in the past ten years. 39/ Managers in Turkey's state manufacturing enterprises earned one-half to one-fifth that of the private sector in 1981 and the net pay has been estimated at not more than $400 a month. In some countries—for example, Benin—SOE salaries are so low that it is accepted practice for managers to take other jobs to earn a sufficient income.

Often, state firms are able to attract capable young executives despite poor pay. In many developing countries small, family-run operations dominate the domestic private sector; hence for many younger executives service in an SOE provides their only chance to run a large business. Employment in a state firm may also serve as a training ground for a private career. This is partly the case in Mexico, for example. Retaining experienced managers when pay is low is more difficult, especially since frequent unjustified interventions and lack of recognition for good performance will also drive away good executives.

In many developing countries top executives of SOEs are recruited from the ranks of the civil service or the military. These individuals often lack the skills to run a commercial venture and may identify more closely with their former bureaucracy than with the enterprise. In Madagascar, for example, SOE managerial positions are dominated by government bureaucrats, who can opt to retain their career positions in the civil service while earning higher pay in the state firms. Some are still paid by their government agencies and receive additional pay from the SOE. This arrangement has been explicitly prohibited for certain SOEs (socialist enterprises and national interest companies) in order to ensure that employees are committed to the enterprise, and the policy for other state firms is currently under review. 40/

The growing number of SOEs has contributed to the shortage of managers in many sub-Saharan African and South Asian countries, a shortage sometimes exacerbated by programs for rapid indigenization. Many senior posts are left vacant or are filled by unqualified staff. For example, in Tanzania half of the ten large agricultural SOEs had no financial manager in 1980, and Nigeria's Electrical Power Authority had thirty-five of its eighty-seven higher management posts vacant in 1981. The lack of competent middle managers often leads the chief executive officer (CEO) to take over lower supervisory functions. In a centralized system the CEOs may also be the only point of contact with outsiders. The organization thus becomes overly dependent on its chief executive and is thus especially vulnerable when CEOs are frequently shifted.

The managers of SOEs typically have a high rate of turnover in developing countries, partly because of shortages as competent people are shifted around to head troubled SOEs, and partly because of political changes. Thus in Peru, CEOs of some public firms change whenever the head of their oversight ministry does (the tenure of ministers in Peru is often less than a year). In Liberia, meanwhile, the average tenure of SOE general managers in the 1970s was less than two years. 41/ Continuity of top management is especially important in a company's formative years. Furthermore, continuity allows a good chief executive time to attract and retain talented middle managers. For example, the Hindustan Machine Tool Company (HMT), one of the most successful Indian SOEs, was also one of the few public corporations in India to have the same chief executive for almost fifteen years. HMT management has consciously stressed continuity, grooming executives for orderly succession. As the HMT experience shows, continuity can be achieved not only by keeping good managers in place for a reasonable period but also by promoting managers from within the firm. Many of the chief executives of Bharat Heavy Electricals Limited, another profitable and dynamic Indian manufacturing company, have come from within the firm.

In certain specialized areas (mining in Zaire, for example), management contracts with expatriate firms have helped alleviate the shortage of managers. Another step is to give priority to managerial development in SOEs. In the past, more attention has been paid to technical expertise for

SOEs than to their managerial requirements. Some of the largest SOEs have their own management centers, but most rely on business schools, management consultants, expatriate advisors, and foreign suppliers or collaborators.

Some countries have taken advantage of the economies of scale in training by creating training centers for groups of enterprises. For example, the Portuguese holding company for manufacturing SOEs, IPE (Instituto dos Participacoes do Estado), provides training to managers of its subsidiaries through a special training wing, CIFAG. CIFAG hires specialized persons as trainers and arranges seminars and workshops. It also arranges for trainees to participate in programs abroad under reciprocal relationships with other training institutes.

"Twinning" an SOE with its counterpart in another country has proved an effective way of transferring know-how and training staff. The more developed SOE may temporarily provide its "twin" with some of its own staff as advisers and trainers, may make periodic visits to give technical assistance, or may employ the staff of its "twin" at its own facility for on-the-job training. A case in point is the Tanzanian Electric Supply Company Limited (TANESCO), which was "twinned" with the Electricity Supply Board (ESB) of Ireland in 1977. A number of TANESCO staff were trained in Dublin, receiving on the job training at ESB or a similar utility. ESB staff also provided technical assistance to TANESCO in Tanzania. Companies offering technical assistance as "twins" are not exclusively from North America and Europe. Among the many examples from developing countries are the Port of Singapore, the National Irrigation Agency of the Philippines, and the Tunisian Water Authority.

Governments sometimes reduce SOE (and private company) access to foreign skills and training by restricting collaboration. This may be understandable in light of difficult foreign exchange shortages, but the damage it can do to an enterprise's training and managerial development should also be considered.

Most SOE managerial training focuses on internal aspects of running a commercial venture, which are similar for public and private firms. Some other programs that are available focus on external aspects of running a state firm. These bring managers and bureaucrats together to discuss the special features of managing SOEs and to train both sides in the areas of conflict resolution, performance evaluation, and the like. In India, the various institutes of management offer seminars for Indian and other executives; elsewhere, the International Center for Public Enterprises at Lubljana, Yugoslavia, and the Harvard Institute for International Development in the United States sponsor workshops.

The administrative burden placed on SOE managers can be relieved by designing projects with an eye to the country's managerial capacity. Typically, new SOEs are created with little or no attention to the managerial problems they may pose. All too often the result is a very large company designed to take advantage of economies of scale and to meet (sometimes overly) optimistic demand forecasts. Such firms require a cadre of skilled executives, which are in short supply. Even when this in not the case, the managers must cope with operating an oversized plant, at least initially. Any savings due to scale may be wiped out, not only by having to operate below capacity with high interest and depreciation charges, but also by the operating inefficiencies that arise when skilled managers are in short supply. A number of problems could be avoided by adapting designs to managerial capacity and by involving the future CEO in an early design stage of the project.

The importance of small size and access to foreign expertise is illustrated by the experiences of HMT. Dr. S.M. Patil, managing director of HMT for fourteen years, attributed much of the company's success to the fact that it started small and had good collaborators. 42/ As Khandwalla notes, "HMT began small, learnt fast, and built on its strengths. Unlike many other Indian public enterprises, HMT was not saddled with a capacity vastly in excess of demand for its products." This meant that HMT could avoid the attendant problems of "excess capacity, high costs, and low earning capability." 43/ Initially HMT relied on its collaborators for training and had more than eighty Swiss experts in the company for an average of five years each. HMT managers also spent an average of nine months with their collaborators in Switzerland--and some stayed even longer. Today HMT is a large, diversified company that exports its expertise in the form of consulting services.

Contributing further to the administrative burden placed on SOE managers is the fact that many are diverted into extraneous activities. In Peru, for example, a public fishing plant runs a hotel. While diversification can be profitable and logical, it is often done for the wrong reasons and, by straining resources, damages the SOE's mainstream activities. Thus, where a state firm has access to funds at low or zero cost and there are few incentives to respond to market forces, inappropriate and inefficient diversification may result. In some cases, such diversion may be at the government's behest or may be the result of pressure from workers. SOEs are often expected to provide hospitals or transport for their staff. The government may require such services from the SOEs rather than expend the effort themselves to improve existing health or transport services. Managers are thus burdened with running these facilities. Moreover, the existing services lose the clientele most able to pay and most likely to pressure for improvements. As a result, the public services may deteriorate further, to the detriment of the poor who are condemned to use them.

VI. Liquidation

By saving the economy from the burden of nonviable enterprises, liquidations act as a major force for efficiency. Because of the financial and social consequences, however, governments are reluctant to let big firms close, whether they are in the public or the private sector. Even when they are small, SOEs are seldom liquidated. But the costs of keeping nonviable companies alive are considerable—fiscally draining, administratively demanding, and wasteful of potentially productive resources. To take an extreme case, in Peru a freeze-drying plant owned by the state was built without adequate study of the market or sufficient skilled staff to operate and maintain the equipment. The supply of raw materials was erratic because of the company's failure to plan its purchases carefully or to pay promptly for delivery. From the start, the firm's production costs exceeded its revenues. It was shut down and reopened on several occasions. Finally, in 1980, and after fifteen years of losses, liquidation procedures began.

This case also illustrates the need for a proper legal framework to allow speedy liquidation. Peruvian law makes it almost impossible to dismiss workers (in both the public and private sectors). Although the company offered its staff a bonus over and above required severance pay to leave, for more than six months after the plant was shut down a small group of workers continued to report for work each day to receive their wages. Until all the staff had left, the assets could not be sold. 44/

Liquidation and other forms of divestment give the government the flexibility to put resources to more productive use. Since these gains have to be weighed against short-term costs, vested interests often deny the state the possibility of even considering the option--to the long-run detriment of the economy.

Bankruptcy of an SOE is not as easy to establish as with a private firm, and even in the private sector the case is often not clear-cut. Unless the government intervenes, a private firm will likely be liquidated when it is insolvent. Insolvency can be straightforward, when a firm is unable to meet its maturing obligations, or it can be a judgment call, when total liabilities exceed the fair and realizable market value of assets. Insolvency, however, is often not a good or sufficient reason for liquidating SOEs--nor is solvency necessarily a good reason for not liquidating. On the one hand, it is not unusual for state firms to be created with 90 or 100 percent debt financing and for the state later to inject equity into the firm by taking over its debt. In this case, the SOE's insolvency reflects the owner's failure to capitalize the project adequately. On the other hand, many public firms are not commercially viable but are solvent because they have access to subsidies or subsidized funds, or enjoy monopoly privileges.

In deciding whether to liquidate, the government needs to determine whether the financial and economic costs of operating the SOE outweigh the benefits. This question obviously raises the ticklish problem of how to measure intangible benefits. Yet in practice many governments are making a determination and closing some of their public companies. The Ivory Coast, for example, has closed sixteen public firms since 1980, and Brazil dissolved ten in 1982.

VII. Divestiture

Selling or denationalizing state-owned enterprises is another way of easing their administrative and financial burden on the state. A working party recommending divestiture in Kenya gave the following reasons:

> First, experience suggests that many of these commerical investments would be more productive, better managed and more profitable in the hands of private owners. ... Second, troubled investments have required an inordinate amount of the time of government administrators, managers and policymakers, hence diverting their attention from the more basic development needs of the nation. Third, many of the initial reasons for these investments have been satisfied or are of lesser importance under present circumstances. 45/

A number of governments, including Bangladesh, Brazil, Chile, Italy, Jamaica, Kenya, the Republic of Korea, Pakistan, Peru, the Philippines, and Zaire, have divested, or are planning to divest, SOEs. Generally, however, the number and importance of the enterprises sold are not large. One exception was Japan. After an initial attempt to promote industrialization through state ownership, the Japanese government in the 1880s sold a large number of state firms, including fifty-two factories, ten mines, and three shipyards.

The most extensive divestiture in more recent times took place in Chile. In 1970 Chile had forty-six SOEs under a holding company, the Production Development Corporation of Chile (CORFO). From 1970 to 1973 the Allende government increased the number of SOEs to 527. Of these, 259 were expropriated by decree, usually because of labor problems. CORFO or its subsidiaries purchased more than 50 percent of the shares in an additional 138 corporations and 14 banks, plus minority interest in another 52 companies and five banks, and acquired extensive agroindustrial assets. The military government that took power in 1973 returned almost all the 259 companies expropriated by decree to their original owners. 46/ Between 1974 and August

1982, CORFO sold its interest in 13 corporations and all but one of the 19 banks, as well as some of the agroindustrial plants and other assets. The total value of the sale was $940 million (See Table 6). 47/

Chile's largest SOEs, which have traditionally been public (such as the electricity company or the petroleum company), were not sold. The net worth of these SOEs was about $11 billion in 1982, compared with the total sale of less than $1 billion. Eight of the ten largest Chilean companies in terms of net worth and five of the largest in terms of sales (in 1979) are public firms. 48/ Chile has more recently sold some small electricity-generating plants and telephone concessions, and plans to sell more; but private interest in purchasing firms in government-dominated sectors has been limited.

Table 6 The Sale of SOEs in Chile, 1974 to August, 1982

	1974	1975	1976	1977	1978	1979	1980	1981	August 1982	Total*
					Values in millions of US$					
Enterprises										
Number	49	28	22	7	8	8	6	3	2	133
Value	3	43	84	94	69	125	22	97	5	$541
Blocks of bank shares										
Number	--	9	4	--	6	1	1	--	--	21
Value	--	170	6	--	41	29	41	--	--	$888
Agroindustrial and other assets										
Value	13	11	17	30	5	11	7	15	3	$112
Total Sales										
Value*	$16	$224	$107	$124	$115	$165	$70	$112	$8	$940

* Totals may not sum due to rounding.
Source: Covan and Voras, 1982.

The sale was by competitive bidding or, if no satisfactory bid was found, through direct negotiations. Most of the sales occurred during 1974-76, when Chile went through a severe recession, which of course affected the sales price. Exactly how much is difficult to ascertain, especially since Chile also experienced extraordinarily high inflation during this period. A more important effect of the timing of the sale was that only very few persons or companies had the funds to buy the enterprises--most were bought by the large industrial groups which had access to foreign credit directly and through their ownership of banks.

As is typical in many developing economies, about twenty groups dominated the financial and industrial scene in Chile in the 1960s. The nationalization and subsequent resale of companies and banks increased the power of these interests by reducing the number of minority shareholders. In 1970, for example, the largest single shareholding in the Banco de Chile, a major private commercial bank, represented only 4.5 percent of the shares outstanding. By 1978 one group held 31 percent of the bank and two others had 10 percent each. The sale of banks and industries to the economic groups thus reinforced the ties between the industrial and financial sectors. There was in practice no separation between the management and the ownership of the enterprises and the banks made sometimes questionable loans to affiliated industries. The banks borrowed heavily abroad and lent domestically at the high market interest rates prevailing in Chile. When the recession hit, many industries could not make their large interest payments and the banks, in turn, could not service their large foreign debt. These circumstances led the government to intervene in several major private banks in 1983.

The sale was quite extensive. As mentioned, the value of the sale was about $1 billion. By comparison, the net worth of the 250 largest Chilean firms in 1978 was less than $4 billion. Nevertheless, the sixty-six SOEs that remain have a combined net worth of about $11 billion and produce close to 18 percent of GDP. 49/ Elsewhere, privatizing programs have been far more limited: Brazil created a commission for divestiture in 1981, and by mid-1982 it had sold ten SOEs and was in the process of selling another thirty-six. Jamaica recently set up a divestiture committee that has sold three enterprises and leased four hotels. Pakistan denationalized some 2,000 rice, flour, and cotton mills; and Bangladesh returned thirty-five jute and twenty-three textile mills to their former private owners in late 1982. The current Peruvian administration, which took office in 1980, has announced its intention to sell its shares in about seventy SOEs over a three-year period.

Divestiture can produce important net gains to society when the costs of public operation outweigh the benefits. It is likely to be easier to ensure genuine competition among private firms and to reduce unjustified government intervention. It could allow the state to concentrate on the most pressing activities that only government can pursue. Nonetheless, divestiture has been hard to implement. It is a politically sensitive measure and prompts charges of corruption. In addition, governments often try to sell only their money losers, for which there are few buyers. Often they also try to sell during a recession when the market is poor. Even profitable nationalized companies may be hard to sell to domestic purchasers. An informal survey of the potential market for Peruvian SOEs found that likely buyers were reluctant to purchase even fairly small profitable companies. The reasons given included fear of renationalization and concern about extensive government regulation of formerly public firms. Many firms were regarded as overmanned and there are strict limits on firing in Peru. These perceptions may compel government to accept a lower price than the market value for a similar private firm. Both Chile and Japan sold most of their state firms on very attractive terms. But accepting a low price may be politically impossible.

There are other difficulties in divesting. The Peruvians, for example, are prohibited from selling SOEs to nationals of countries outside the Andean Group, a restriction that substantially reduces the potential market. In addition, large traditionally public firms are almost impossible to sell. Most such firms are monopolies and are likely to be subject to extensive government regulation regardless of who is the owner. The fact that they are highly visible may also make private buyers wary.

Another obstacle in developing countries is the absence of a strong capital market. Since many public companies are large, or the government may wish to sell a large number of smaller firms, domestic investors may not be able to raise enough capital to buy them. For example, a study of the proposed sale of Peruvian SOEs estimated the market value of the government shares to be about $500 million or 3 percent of 1982 GDP and one-fourth of domestic quasi-money. 50/ It would require a fairly substantial change in domestic portfolio preferences to absorb these shares unless the government offers very liberal financing terms. Finally, as the Chilean experience shows, selling SOEs to oligopolists who already dominate the private sector could result in unhealthy ties between financial institutions and industry.

Efforts to develop the stock market, and schemes that appeal to small savers through their pension funds, could make it easier for governments to divest. Spreading ownership more widely and divesting only gradually could improve the chances of privatization, and might even reduce the political controversy involved. A sale to many small shareholders might make a realistically low price more acceptable. Leasing can also be a promising route to divestiture: a private manager might be brought in to run a potentially profitable enterprise for a share of the profits and an option to buy.

VIII. Alternatives to State Ownership

The development of the state-owned sector is seldom the result of a carefully conceived scheme. Rather, this sector evolves in response to a variety of circumstances through the nationalization of foreign companies, the takeover of failing firms, and the creation of SOEs to answer a felt economic or social need. But ownership is only one possible mechanism for achieving government's aims. A list of alternatives to state-owned firms in manufacturing, marketing, public utilities, and mining is given in Table 7.

Most of these alternatives rely on private enterprise, which in many developing countries means small traders and farmers, plus a few large foreign firms. Thus, the authorities may see little alternative to state ownership to promote development while keeping economic power in domestic hands. Yet these alternatives merit consideration. Circumstances change and as a country's economy develops there may be opportunities to replace an SOE with regulated domestic private firms. Experience has taught that the difficulty of directing an SOE can be as great as or greater than that of regulating a private firm. Many governments today find themselves overtaxed and may be able to achieve their goals using a mechanism that is less bureaucratically demanding than an SOE.

Each of the alternatives to state ownership has advantages and disadvantages. For example, fiscal measures might be used instead of a public manufacturing company to encourage industrialization where the private sector is thought to be too risk averse. Studies of industrial zones have shown,

Table 7 The Main Alternatives to SOEs in Selected Sectors

Principal objectives	Main Alternatives

Manufacturing

1. Promote industrialization, particularly in capital intensive sectors, or those deemed "strategic"--where domestic private sector lacks capital or entrepreneurial skills and drive

   Regulation of foreign enterprise, joint ventures, investment guarantees, fiscal incentives, credit measures, promotion of capital market

2. Replace foreign with national control

   Management or construction contracts

3. Control monopolies

   Regulation of private enterprise, antitrust regulation or import liberalization

4. Establish stable and uniform prices, or subsidize prices to consumer for basic needs or to producer for essential inputs.

   Price stabilization funds, subsidies, price controls

5. Promote employment

   Provide or promote training, fiscal incentives, measures to promote labor mobility

6. Capture revenues or foreign exchange for state

   Revenue measures

Marketing Boards

1. Establish stable and uniform prices

   Price controls, stabilization funds

2. Subsidize price paid by consumer for basic needs or by producer for essential input

   Price controls or price subsidies, income support

3. Bargain more effectively in international markets

   Producer cooperatives

4. Protect small farmer from gouging by middleman

   Regulation of private traders, cooperatives

Table 7 The Main Alternatives to SOEs in Selected Sectors (Continued)

Principal objectives	Main Alternatives

Public utility

1. Control natural monopoly

2. Ensure adequate and
    efficient provision of a
    basic service
                                                Promotion and regulation of private
    industry, management contracts

3. Ensure necessary expansion
    of service requiring large,
    lumpy investments to avoid
    bottlenecks to growth

4. National control of basic
    service

Mining Company

1. National control over
    exhaustible, strategic
    resource   Regulation of private industry

2. Capture rents in order to
    increase government revenue
    or redistribute income   Revenue measures

3. Ensure rational and efficient
    exploitation to generate
    maximum rents and foreign
    exchange for country's
    development   Regulation of private industry

4. Control externalities
    (e.g., pollution)   Regulation of private industry

however, that tax exemptions or financial incentives may play a very limited role in attracting investments and may be overgenerous or given when the investment would have occurred anyway. 51/ Furthermore, fiscal incentives can result in a serious misallocation of resources. Rebates of tariffs on imported capital goods, for example, can cause overly capital intensive production with low domestic value added. Governments may impose a minimum value added requirement to try to avoid these problems, but this involves reporting and investigation that add to the administrative costs, over and above the fiscal costs. Many such measures eventually become a permanent crutch rather than a temporary incentive.

Credit incentives may be used to encourage private industrialists lacking funds, but they can also cause serious distortions. In addition, rationed credit and subsidized interest rates repress financial markets. Credit guarantees can result in overly indebted industries and place the government's own finances at risk.

Another alternative is to promote the capital market through regulation to increase information, protect the small investor, and prevent fraud. Schemes to tap new savings can also be effective. However, this is a long-run solution that offers little immediate hope to the least developed countries.

An SOE is a more immediate solution, but it also creates the likelihood of distortions. SOE access to subsidized credit and government guarantees, for example, results in overly capital intensive production, crowds out other industries, and increases government debt. Moreover, it can be a fiscal drain and an administrative burden. And, like tax or credit incentives, public firms are hard to get rid of once they have outlived their usefulness. Thus the choice is between a range of imperfect solutions.

Experience has shown in far too many cases that an investment that proves difficult to promote in the private sector may indeed be a poor investment. The risks and expenses that the private sector shunned often become the downfall of the SOE, and the expected social benefits fall far short of the unexpected costs.

One common reason for creating SOEs is to control monopolies but this assumes that the SOE will be effectively controlled and efficiently managed. In some cases an alternative is to eliminate the monopoly by breaking up large domestic groups or reducing tariff barriers. When the monopoly is a natural one, almost all countries have opted for state ownership. The most notable exception to this is the United States, where many utilities are regulated private firms. The results have been mixed. One study of the cost structures and prices of similar publicly owned and regulated private electricity companies in the United States in the 1960s found that average prices and costs were significantly higher in the private than in the public firms. 52/ The causes of the different cost structures are hard to evaluate since the SOEs may be able to purchase inputs at lower prices and have a different wage scale.

In some circumstances public monopolies exist where competitive private firms could operate. For example, research on cities that allow small competitive bus companies show that they often provide a faster, better service without subsidies at the same fares as the money-losing public service. In three cities (Calcutta, Istanbul, and Bangkok) where public and private operators compete at the same fares, the public buses all had losses, whereas the private ones paid taxes and earned a profit. 53/ In Calcutta, for example, the Calcutta State Transport Corporation (CSTC) requires a subsidy of US$1 million a month. Private buses operating without subsidy account for two-thirds of all trips. The success of the private companies has been attributed to quicker repairs (only half of CSTC's buses are generally running), better fare collection (evasion of CSTC fares is estimated at 25 percent) and higher labor productivity (CSTC employed thirty staff per bus in 1980, one of the highest staffing levels in the world). 54/

From the early 1940s to the early 1960s, Buenos Aires first had a large private, then public, bus company with limited private competition. Initially the intention was to make this firm a monopoly; but by 1959 the public company's annual losses totaled about US$44 million and in 1962 it was dissolved. Today, there are fifty private firms. Fares are set by the state but many routes coincide, and there is strong quality competition. As a result, the buses are well maintained, service is frequent with little waiting, and 94 percent of the routes have service for at least eighteen hours a day. 55/

One arguent used against private bus service is that bus operators pursuing profits would not serve poorer communities or work during off-peak hours. Yet, in cities like Bangkok, Calcutta, Hong Kong, Istanbul, and Nairobi minibuses are the only transportation service to many low-income communities, especially illegal squatter areas or centers with narrow streets. Their smaller size also allows them to work during off-peak hours and still earn a profit.

Private bus companies are also criticized for keeping driver incomes low. Many of the drivers, however, earn more than they could in other occupations. Empirical evidence is limited, but it suggests that drivers earn better than the average household income in Istanbul and Calcutta.

Other abuses attributed to competition--that it increases congestion, noise, and pollution--can be corrected through regulation. If the government wished to subsidize fares for low-income groups, it could provide free or discounted tickets to such groups rather than operate a public service to keep all fares low.

In the absence of competition, most municipal bus services have little incentive to respond to consumer preference. Their rates are set and, if need be, subsidized; competition from minibuses is usually outlawed or highly regulated; and demand is seen as inelastic. The experience with competition shows that concern about profits results in better service; equipment is better maintained and more quickly repaired; and a fiscal drain is eliminated.

Whether it is easier to police an SOE or a regulated private firm is by no means clear. Some argue that the state firm provides government with much more information on the workings of the industry than a private firm would. Yet governments in most developing countries have very little information on their SOEs. Even in a relatively sophisticated economy like Brazil, the ability of central authorities to regulate or even be kept informed about their enterprises can be quite limited. In the United States, meanwhile, it has been easier to force private firms to comply with government pollution controls than the publicly owned Tennessee Valley Authority. Since in developing countries the private alternative to a large SOE is likely to be a foreign company, the problems of regulation are compounded. Nevertheless, some countries have been able to employ foreign firms successfully with management contracts, which offer an alternative to SOEs that will keep state control and tap private management skills. Operation and maintenance of the water and sewerage service in the Ivory Coast, for example, is provided by a private company, Societe de Distribution d'Eau de La Cote d'Ivoire (SODECI). SODECI was originally started by a French water supply company; today 52 percent of its shareholders are Ivorians. Although the company still depends heavily on expatriates, the general manager and the provincial managers are Ivorians.

Despite its rapid expansion, the water system in the Ivory Coast is one of the best in West Africa. The system is well designed, equipped, maintained, and operated. Water quality and pressure are uniformly good. Service is metered and water losses are low. Water tariffs are set to cover SODECI's fee plus debt service. By setting rates to cover costs fully, the Ivory Coast can finance its high standard of service. Rates are among the highest in Africa because consumers rather than taxpayers pay for the service they receive. Rates for small users are low, so the poor can afford the service. The planning and construction of all new investments are done by a unit in the Ministry of Public Works, which also supervises SODECI. The institutional separation of new investment from operations makes it easier to evaluate SODECI's results and ensures government control over the expansion of the system.

The management contract has allowed the Ivory Coast to ensure top-calibre management of its water and sewerage system. As a private company, SODECI is free (within the contracted limits) to hire, fire, and compensate its staff. This freedom, plus a strong emphasis on training (SODECI is the only water supply company in West Africa with its own training center), enables the company to attract, train, and keep qualified personnel. An SOE would have had difficulty matching SODECI's salaries and training budget.

Management contracts do not relieve the government of the problems of supervision any more than does an SOE. In the case of the Ivory Coast, SODECI is paid a fee related to the volume of water sold. This fee is calculated on the basis of agreed standards for staff, equipment, energy, and other inputs,

plus a margin based on agreed overheads and profits, indexed against
inflation. During the periodic review of tariffs, the government has an
opportunity to scrutinize SODECI's costs carefully; in the intervening period
SODECI has a strong incentive to minimize its costs.

The success of management contracts thus depends on the skills of the
supervisory agency as well as on the talents of the concessionary. The
government must be sufficiently informed to be able to set prices that allow
reasonable profits and attract competent firms. Although it may not be easier
to supervise a private firm than an SOE, it is easier to change firms.

IX. Agenda for Reform

This report has suggested ways of improving SOE efficiency by
concentrating on the problems that are common to most SOEs in most
countries. It has examined how the reality of SOEs differs from the
theoretical ideal on the basis of what is known about the ideal conditions for
operating efficiently. By recognizing the SOEs' special circumstances and
constraints, developing countries should be able to develop an agenda for
reform that would correct some of their main weaknesses:

● Setting clear cut and attainable objectives is the inescapable first
step toward improved SOE performance. The costs of noncommercial constraints
placed on SOEs should be calculated and weighed against the benefits to
society.

● Once contraints have been identified and the costs estimated,
governments can instruct many SOEs to maximize their profits, taking into
account other objectives that reduce profits by reimbursing the companies or
lowering their profit targets.

● Negotiated agreements, such as contracts or corporate plans, can help to put SOE-government relations on a more constructive plane. In particular, two-way contracts can help win SOE management over to the idea of reform by setting out benefits as well as responsibilities. Once government has laid down objectives, managers can be made responsible for choosing the methods of achieving them.

● Systems for monitoring and evaluating performance are needed to transform good intentions into results. By promoting domestic and international competition, encouraging consumers and other customers to make their views known, and requiring SOEs to pay the opportunity costs of their capital, governments can add to the pressures for good SOE performance.

● Managerial ability is key to the success of SOE reform. Managerial incentives linked to performance are important in motivating top managers. Some of the most powerful incentives are nonpecuniary (recognition, prestige, awards). Compensation and training should be geared toward creating a corps of competent SOE managers with appropriate skills. Efforts should also be directed at encouraging continuity of senior staff.

● The managerial and fiscal burden of SOEs can be reduced by liquidating nonviable enterprises as well as by selective sales and by using alternative means to achieve the government's goals. These should not be treated as instant solutions, but rather as integral parts of the process of replacing the burden of central administration by decentralized market forces.

With strong political backing, this agenda is feasible. In any administrative system there are strong vested interests opposed to change. Opposition to reform may come from managers of powerful SOEs or senior government bureaucracts fearing loss of power, labor unions fearing job cuts, SOE clients fearing an end to subsidized outputs, suppliers fearing reduced

SOE spending, or even SOE competitors (some private companies profit nicely when prices or incentives for a sector are geared to allow an inefficient SOE to survive).

Since these elements are interrelated, a piecemeal approach is unlikely to achieve the desired results. Without clear objectives there can be no standards by which to judge performance; without accountability few governments would increase SOE autonomy; autonomy becomes license without performance evaluation; incentives can be linked to performance only if there is a meaningful way to measure results; performance evaluation makes sense only if managers have the autonomy to influence outcomes; without performance evaluation there is no way to distinguish good managers from bad. Developing a framework to guide SOEs toward efficiency is thus a lengthy, complex process that requires commitment, persistence, and flexibility on the part of the state authorities and enterprise management.

Footnotes

1/ The countries are Argentina, Bolivia, Colombia, India, Korea, Malta, Nepal, Paraguay, Tanzania, Tunisia, Turkey, and Venezuela. Data derived from Peter Short, "Appraising the Role of Public Enterprises, an International Comparison." IMF Occasional Paper Series, Washington, D.C., 1983. Averages weighted by GDP.

2/ Algeria, Argentina, Brazil, Burma, Chile, Costa Rica, India, Ivory Coast, Kenya, Korea, Malawi, Malta, Mexico, Pakistan, Panama, Paraguay, Peru, Portugal, the Philippines, Sri Lanka, Tanzania, Thailand, Turkey, Uruguay, and Venezuela. Figures are averages weighted by gross fixed capital formation. Source: P. Short, "Appraising the Role of Public Enterprises."

3/ Contribution averaged 9.6 percent of GDP about 1974-77 in seven developed countries (Australia, Austria, France, Germany, Italy, the Netherlands, and the United Kingdom).

4/ Leroy Jones and Edward S. Mason, "The Role of Economic Factors in Determining the Size and Structure of the Public Enterprise Sector in Mixed Economy LDCs," in Public Enterprise in Less Developed Countries, Leroy Jones, ed. (Cambridge: Cambridge University Press, 1982).

5/ Data on SOE capital stock are scanty, and differences in accounting practices and, in particular, in the revaluation of assets for inflation make it impossible to generalize about returns.

6/ Derived from P. Short, "Appraising the Role of Public Enterprises."

7/ Calculated as operating receipts (excluding subsidies from the central government) less operating expenditures (including an estimated depreciation allowance) divided by operating revenues plus operating expenditures (excluding depreciation). Operating revenues plus operating expenditures represents SOE "activity" and is used as a base rather than net fixed assets because of the different practices in revaluing assets and calculating depreciation. See A. Gantt II and G. Dutto, "Financial Performance of Government-Owned Corporations in Less Developed Countries," International Monetary Fund Staff Papers vol. 25, (Washington, D.C. 1968) pp. 102-42.

8/ Derived from data in P. Short, "Appraising the Role of Public Enterprises."

9/ World Bank, Borrowing in International Capital Markets (Washington, D.C., 1980 and 1981).

10/ For example, a study of Australia's two airlines found higher productivity in the private firm than in the public one, although both are required by law to use similar equipment and fly the same routes; see D.G. Davis, "The Efficiency of Public Versus Private Firms: The Case of Australia's Two Airlines," Journal of Law and Economics (April 1971). Another study found similar levels and trends in total factor productivity in the Canadian public and private railways; see D.W. Caves and L.R. Christensen, "The Relative Efficiency of Public and Private Firms in a Competitive Environment: The Case of Canadian Railways," Journal of Political Economy (October 1980).

11/ Based on World Bank data. The evidence suggests that these trends were not due to changes in the product mix.

12/ Anne Krueger and Baran Tuncer, Estimating Total Factor Productivity Growth in a Developing Country, World Bank Staff Working Paper no. 422 (Washington, D.C., October 1980).

13/ See Leroy P. Jones, "Public Enterprise for Whom? Perverse Distributional Consequences of Public Operational Decisions," paper read at the Conference of Problems and Policies of Industrialization in an Open Economy, at Bogazici University, Istanbul, Turkey, August 20-24, 1981.

14/ USAID, "Egypt's Food and Energy Subsidies in 1979" (Cairo, undated), in Jones, "Perverse Distributional Consequences," p.6.

15/ Value added assumes an ICOR of 3:1. Jones, "Perverse Distributional Consequences," p.13.

16/ See Geoffrey Lamb and Linda Muller, Control, Accountability, and Incentives in a Successful Development Institution: The Kenya Tea Development Authority, World Bank Staff Working Paper no. 550 (Washington, D.C., 1982).

17/ World Bank, "The Railways Problem" (Washington, D.C., January 28, 1982). Restricted circulation document for internal use only.

18/ Brazil had 560 parastatals in 1979, including nonprofit foundations and quasi-governmental service agencies, of which about 355 conform to the definition of an SOE used in this report. See Secretariat for Control of State Enterprises (Planning Secretariat), State Enterprises in Brazil and the Control of the SEST: Background and 1980 Results (Brasilia, 1981).

19/ See Romano Prodi, "Economic Performance and Political Problems of Public Industrial Firms in Italy." Forthcoming World Bank Staff Working Paper.

20/ H. U. Beg, Aamer Raza Khan, D. M. Qureshi, A. Kalam, and Anwar H. Siddiqui, "Report of the Implementation Committee on the Reorganization of State Industrial Enterprises, November 1978," in Leroy Jones, Efficiency of Public Manufacturing Enterprises in Pakistan (August 1981).

21/ See Peter Knight, Economic Reforms in Socialist Countries: The Experiences of China, Hungary, Romania, and Yugoslavia, World Bank Staff Working Paper no. 586 (Washington, D.C., 1983).

22/ See, for example, BPE, Public Enterprise Survey, 1980-81, vols. I-III (New Delhi, 1982).

23/ See Bureau of Public Enterprises, "Performance Aims and Financial Targets of Central Government Public Enterprises, 1982/83 and 1983/84" (New Delhi, 1982).

24/ World Bank, "Arab Republic of Egypt: Issues of Trade Strategy and Investment Planning" (Washington, D.C., January 14, 1983). Restricted circulation document for internal use only.

25/ The Financial and Economic Obligations of the Nationalized Industries (London, April 1961). This discussion refers to the major nationalized industries: Post Office and Telecommunications, Electricity Industry, British Gas, British Railways, National Bus Company, National Freight Company, National Coal Board, British Steel Corporation, and British Railway Board.

26/ See United Kingdom, House of Commons, Financing of the Nationalized Industries, Eighth Report from the Treasury and Civil Service Committee, Session 1980-81, 27 July 1981.

27/ P. Knight, "Economic Reforms in Socialist Countries."

28/ David Williams, "The Choice of Technology and National Planning: The Case of Tanzania," unpublished DBA thesis, Harvard University Graduate School of Business Administration, 1975.

29/ World Bank files.

30/ "Inflation Scoreboard," Business Week, May 2, 1983. Sales and dividends adjusted for change in CPI. Profits calculated after adjusting operating costs for changes in the CPI and calculating depreciation on the inflation-adjusted value of inventories, plant, and equipment.

31/ Richard D. Mallon, "Public Enterprise versus Other Methods of State Intervention as Instruments of Redistribution Policy: the Malaysian Experience," in Public Enterprise in Less Developed Countries, ed. Jones (Cambridge: Cambridge University Press, 1982).

32/ World Bank and IFC, "Peru: The Management and Sale of State-owned Enterprises" (Washington, D.C., August 27, 1982). Restricted circulation document for internal use only.

33/ P. Knight, "Economic Reforms in Socialist Countries," p. 80.

34/ Pradip N. Khandwalla, "The Performance Determinants of Public Enterprises: Case Studies of Four Equipment Manufacturing Indian Public Enterprises," forthcoming in the World Bank Staff Working Paper Series.

35/ John Redwood and John Hatch, Controlling Public Industries (Oxford: Basil Blackwell, 1982) p. 61.

36/ World Bank files.

37/ P. Knight, "Economic Reforms in Socialist Countries."

38/ Ibid.

39/ World Bank, "Turkey: Industrialization and Trade Strategy" (Washington, D.C., February 18, 1982). Restricted circulation document for internal use only.

40/ World Bank, "Turkey: Issues and Options in the Energy Sector" (Washington, D.C., March, 1983). Restricted circulation document for internal use only.

41/ World Bank files.

42/ In a speech at Bangalore, India, to a seminar sponsored by the Indian Institute of Management at Ahmedabad on July 14, 1982. Others also cite the importance of Dr. Patil's role in stressing growth, efficiency, and managerial competence at HMT.

43/ Khandwalla, "The Performance Determinants of Public Enterprises."

44/ World Bank and IFC, "Peru: The Management and Sale of State-owned Enterprises."

45/ Republic of Kenya, Report and Recommendations of the Working Party on Government Expenditures (Philip Ndegwa, Chairman), July 1982.

46/ Owners of the returned enterprises were required to assume any debts incurred by the firms during state ownership and to drop any lawsuits relating to their property claims that they may have instigated against the state.

47/ Presentation of General Don Luis Covian and Enrique Matte Voras (Manager of Normalization at CORFO) to the Seminar on Public Enterprises, Brazil, September 1982. See also CORFO, Office of the Manager of Normalization of Enterprises, "Return of Enterprises and Assets to Private Ownership, 1973-78," (undated).

48/ World Bank, "Chile: Economic Memorandum" (Washington, D.C. 1981). Restricted circulation document for internal use only.

49/ Covian and Voras, Seminar on Public Enterprises.

50/ World Bank and IFC, "Peru: The Management and Sale of State-Owned Enterprises."

51/ See UNIDO, International Center for Industrial Studies, "Export Processing Zones in Developing Countries," August, 1980.

52/ Robert A. Meyer, "Publicly Owned versus Privately Owned Utilities: A Policy Choice," Review of Economics and Statistics, vol. 57 no. 4, (November 1975).

53/ Charles Feibel and A.A. Walters, "Ownership and Efficiency in Urban
     Buses" (September 1979; processed). See also A.A. Walters, Costs and
     Scale of Bus Services, World Bank Staff Working Paper no. 325
     (Washington, D.C., April, 1979).

54/ Gabriel Roth and George G. Wynne, Learning From Abroad, Free Enterprise
     Urban Transportation. (New Brunswick, N.J.: Transaction Books, 1982).

55/ John Hibbs, "Urban Bus Transport in Buenos Aires--The 'Colectivos'"
     (N.d.; processed).

Annex A

Contracts between the State and its Enterprises:
The Experience of France and Senegal

I. France 1/

Contracts between the government and its enterprises began in France in the late 1960s. A working group on improving the structure and operating conditions of SOEs suggested "program contracts" as a way to establish "the intentions and reciprocal commitments of the State and the enterprises' management." 2/ Two contracts were concluded on the basis of the group's recommendations: with the French State Railways (SNCF) and the electricity company, Electricite de France (EDF).

A second working group in the mid-1970s again recommended contracts with the fifteen largest state enterprises in order to clarify state-enterprise relations. 3/ Only four contracts resulted: with Air France and the coal company, Charbounages de France (CDF), in 1978; with the shipping

---

1/ Much of this section is based on P. Amouyel, "Contractual Relations between the State and the Public Sector: The French Experience with Contracts Concluded with Public Enterprises," draft background paper prepared for the World Bank (November 12, 1982, Original: French). See also Jean-Pierre C. Anastassopoulos, "The French Experience: Conflicts with Government," in State-owned Enterprise in the Western Economies, ed. Raymond Vernon and Yair Aharoui, (New York: St. Martin's Press, 1981) and "La Strategiedes enterprises publiques (background paper prepared for the Dailoz, 1980).

2/ Nora Report (Rapport sur les entreprises publiques, La Documentation Francoise, Paris, 1968).

3/ Report of a working group chaired by Mr. Renaud de la Geniere (March 1977).

firm, Compagnie Generale Maritime (CGM) in 1979; and a second contract with the railways in 1979.

Contracts gained renewed popularity in 1981 with the expansion of the state-owned sector. The Interim National Plan for 1982-83 called for "contract plans" to set out a framework for the SOEs consistent with the national plans, and to provide full management autonomy to the newly nationalized companies within these rules of the game. As of March 1983, eight contracts had been signed with the principal SOEs operating in competitive markets and three more were expected to be signed shortly (signatories include Renault, Machines Bull, Usinor, and Thomson). In addition, contracts are being negotiated with the traditional SOEs, notably the electricity company, the railways, Air France, and the Coal and Gas company.

The earlier "program contracts" concentrated especially on the investment program while the 1983 "plan contracts" are expected to be more comprehensive in scope and more closely coordinated with the national development plan.

Characteristics of the Program Contracts

The contracts covered a three- to five-year period and were based on the government's macroeconomic projections for the development plan and the SOEs' corporate plans. Each SOE pledged itself to meet investment and operational targets. For example, in its 1979-82 contract, SNCF promised to achieve increases of 2.7 percent annually in passenger kilometers and 1.4 percent in ton kilometers, to improve the quality of service (including regularity, comfort, and scheduling in response to demand), to increase labor productivity from 522,000 kilometer-units of traffic per employee in 1977 to 605,000 in 1980, and to carry out the agreed investment program. For its part, the state's obligations included not only investment finance but also prior compensation for costs associated with public service obligations. Air France was to be compensated for having to operate the Caravelle IIIs and to split operations between two Paris airports; SNCF was to be subsidized for operating lines with low traffic density; CDF was to be compensated for giving preference to French coal. The government also pledged to increase the autonomy of the SOEs. This included greater freedom to set rates within certain limits and greater autonomy in investment programming and internal reorganization.

Finally, the contracts require the SOE to provide data on its progress in achieving the targets, and provide for consultations should either party fail to fulfill its bargain or if economic circumstances differ substantially from the forecasts.

Results of the Contracts

The first two contracts were disrupted by the 1973 oil shock, which nullified their forecasts. The subsequent inflation and slowdown in growth led the authorities to curtail the pricing freedom promised in the contracts and expand the tasks assigned to the SOEs without providing adequate compensation. As a result, few of the financial targets were met. The second group of contracts met a somewhat similar fate following the 1979 oil shock. Again, rate increases did not always keep pace with costs and promised pricing freedom was restricted.

Nevertheless, the contracts contributed to a number of improvements in the individual SOEs. Although the financial goals were not always met, the SOEs' financial positions were improved by the policy of state subsidies for social service obligations. Many internal improvements were also achieved: for example, SNCF reached its worker productivity targets during most of the years of its contract (1970-75); EDF exceeded its total factor productivity targets for 1971-75; SNCP reorganized its operations; and EDF decentralized some of its activities as pledged in the contracts. Moreover, the refinement of corporate planning and the introduction of management audits contributed to better managerial control within the SOEs.

The contracts also contributed to a loosening of a priori government controls. For example, prior controls on real estate operations by EDF or on internal reorganization of SNCF were eased. State financing for investments covered by the contract became more automatic. Some enterprises were given control over their profits and greater access to financial markets.

II. Senegal 4/

Senegal's government has negotiated contracts with five state-owned enterprises since 1980 and is in the process of negotiating five more. Although it is too early to draw any firm conclusions, initial results are promising and suggest some lessons for other developing countries.

The initial impetus for negotiating the contracts came from the prime minister. The SOE managers quickly saw a number of advantages in the contracts and were supportive. The technical ministries and the Ministry of Finance were less enthusiastic, rightly viewing the contracts as a curb on their power over the SOEs.

The contracts were modeled on the French example and the process was set up with advisers from the French government. The contracts were initially drafted by the SOE, then discussed by a negotiating committee consisting of

---

4/ Based on a background paper by Barbara Bruns (World Bank Staff member) and Bank files.

representatives of the company, the oversight ministries, and the prime minister's office. An interministerial meeting chaired by the prime minister was called to resolve any major issues that the negotiators could not. To date, contracts have been concluded with three transport companies (the railways, airline, and bus companies) and two rural development agencies.

Characteristics of the Contracts

Like their French counterparts, the Senegalese contracts specify the mutual commitments of the state and the SOE. They spell out the enterprise's objectives and quantify its performance targets for the next three years. For example, Air Senegal pledged to balance its books by FY 1983/84, keep expenditures from growing by more than 8 percent a year, and increase traffic by 5 percent a year. The government, for its part, committed itself to a formula for tariff increases, investment financing, repayment of arrears, and operating subsidies. Again, as in France, subsidies are provided on the basis of the philosophy that the state should reimburse the SOE for the cost of its public service obligations. Thus, Air Senegal will be reimbursed for its money-losing public service lines.

The contracts took a long time to prepare, as much as two years in some cases, and the quality varied considerably. The burden of preparation fell almost wholly on the SOEs and the results depended on the complexity of operations, the calibre of information available, and the skill of the SOE team in diagnosing problems and identifying the measures required for improved performance.

Results of the Contracts

The preparation of the contracts forced the SOEs to do strategic planning, to identify the sources of their operating deficits, and articulate their medium-term operating and investment goals, often for the first time. Air

Senegal and the Dakar bus company, for example, calculated losses per passenger-km on services the government obliged them to operate for the first time. All the companies had to prepare detailed three-year projections of production and worker productivity targets, cash flows, and investment execution. All the enterprises underwent full-scale audits, although some audits were only completed during negotiations. Contracts thus generated a great deal of useful information on the SOEs and provided a valuable exercise in strategic planning.

The contract negotiations allowed the government to compare more systematically the cost of social objectives and investment proposals with their benefits. As a result, loss-making air services to certain remote areas were cut back. The government also reconsidered a costly investment in passenger rail equipment after the railway's plan presented a thorough quantification of its long-term implications for the company's debt service and operating revenues. Ultimately, senior ministers decided to concentrate new investment on freight, rather than passenger, traffic. The government also adopted formulae for regular tariff adjustments linked to increases in the costs of inputs (especially fuel) for most enterprises. It agreed to place limits on staff numbers to protect enterprises from pressures to take on excess or ill-qualified personnel.

Some of the contracts have produced measurable improvements in SOE performance. For example, the bus company, SOTRAC, has been guaranteed regular tariff increases, quarterly payment of a specific subsidy for money-losing suburban lines, and financial support for more buses and a second maintenance terminal. For its part, the company has set strict targets for worker productivity, maintenance, and more efficient fleet utilization--targets which, so far, it has met. Improvements in cash flow alone enabled

SOTRAC to eliminate its bank overdraft and 30 percent of its arrears to suppliers in the first year of the contract.

The results of the contracts with the agricultural SOEs have been less encouraging than those in the transport sector. In part this is because climatic conditions and world price fluctuations negated the projections, and the SOEs' commitments were then ignored rather than revised. Contracts may be less well suited to rural development enterprises because of their greater vulnerability to unpredictable exogenous changes and the greater difficulty of quantifying targets.

The least successful contract was with one of the rural development enterprises in need of serious restructuring. It proved politically impossible to reach agreement on the major changes required to restore the company's finances--including deep cuts in staff and overhead, radical changes in production methods, and greater cost recovery from farmers. Not surprisingly, SOE managers are disinclined to propose drastic reductions in operations or to repudiate their past decisions, and the pressure for consensus during negotiations militates against imposition of radical changes. This illustrates a combined weakness and strength of the contracts. Because of the stress on negotiated agreement, neither party can impose changes where there is strong resistance. For the same reason, the changes that are agreed to are more likely to be taken seriously.

One grave weakness of the Senegelese contracts was the failure to estimate the global financial constraints or the total indirect as well as direct cost of the SOEs to the Treasury. As a result, they commit the government to an unrealistically high level of financing. This has reduced the pressure to limit SOEs' operating deficits or to set priorities for investments and trim accordingly. Many of the contracts increased rather than decreased the levels of subsidies in real terms, even though one of the main objectives of the exercise was to relieve the SOE drain on the budget.

The Government has since begun to develop a consistent set of realistic macroeconomic assumptions for the contracts. A study is underway to estimate total indirect as well as direct subsidies that could make a sizable difference. SOTRAC's exemption from taxes on fuel and imported vehicles, for example, has been estimated to be equivalent to 50 percent of its direct operating subsidies.

Another major omission had been the failure to monitor performance seriously and to develop incentives or sanctions linked to results. The Senegalese government has since instituted six-month joint reviews of contract execution to examine why targets have not been met and to revise the contract if necessary. The next step would be to develop incentives linked to performance.

Lessons of Experience

The experience of Senegal provides some useful lessons for implementing contracts in developing countries:

- High-level political commitment is essential. Contracts provoke powerful enemies, particularly in the ministries that will lose some of their power.

- Without a consistent and feasible set of assumptions, the contracts become an intellectual exercise. The targets of the firm and the government's financial commitments must recognize real constraints and be based on a realistic appreciation of the future. The financial and administrative implications of the contracts must be spelled out and integrated into the budget and national plan. Investments should be evaluated in terms of global priorities and constraints and not just on a project-by-project basis.

● Even the most realistic projection can be overtaken by events. The contracts should be revised as circumstances change. For primary product producers, especially where exogenous factors like climate and world price fluctuations play heavily in production targets, such flexibility is essential.

● Procedures for monitoring results and incentives or sanctions linked to performance are an essential part of the contract process.

● Technical assistance and training may be needed to implement comprehensive audits and to help prepare the SOE corporate plans. It may be preferable to begin with simpler, less ambitious plans to reduce the cost and time of preparation.

III. Conclusions

Although the extent and success of contracts to date has been limited, the idea keeps resurfacing and the present government of France has made it a major tool of SOE policy. Contracts have several advantages that account for their enduring appeal.

- They force the state and the enterprise to set out their
  intentions clearly, to transform vague targets into
  quantifiable goals. This also forces the enterprise to
  develop a comprehensive corporate plan as the basis for
  negotiations and requires the government to clarify its
  objectives. Both parties are forced to plan for the
  medium as well as the short term and to think and act
  more consistently.

- They allow the negotiators to anticipate areas of
  potential conflict, work out disagreements beforehand,
  and set up procedures for resolving future conflicts.

- They establish the two-way nature of state-SOE relations,
  setting out the mutual obligations of each party.

- They often produce the first quantification of the cost
  of using SOEs to achieve government's broader policy
  objectives.

Contracts between the state and its enterprises are amorphous
documents, not really legally binding on either party. In France the state
did not always keep its end of the bargain; in Senegal some of the SOEs failed
in their commitments. In both countries the important benefits of the
contracts came not from the documents themselves, but from the process of
preparation, negotiation, and revision. This process can be lengthy and
costly. It took about two years to prepare the contract for Senegal's railway
and the Air France contract negotiations took 26 months. Because preparation
and negotiation are so cumbersome, the contracts are vulnerable in times of
crisis when governments search for a "quick fix." For the same reason,
critics question whether contracts have too high a transaction cost to be a

useful tool. Yet this disadvantage could be a benefit, if the negotiators--
who are also the implementors--were strongly motivated to assure the success
of their contract since they have invested considerable time and effort in it.

Contracts are most likely to be effective when they are linked with
comprehensive reforms of the SOE environment. Measures to eliminate price
distortions, expand competition, select and train SOE managers with commercial
skills, selectively reduce government subsidies, and the like are integral to
the success of. the microreforms introduced by the contracts.

Annex B

The Pakistan Signaling System 1/

In 1981 Pakistan's Ministry of Production launched a project to improve the performance of the SOEs under its jurisdiction. The minister announced that no major new investment projects would be allocated to the enterprises until they had proved themselves capable of making efficient use of their existing resources. (The public firms had absorbed more than 70 percent of total public and private investment in manufacturing in 1980). He announced a goal of increasing SOE operating efficiency by 5 percent a year, which is estimated to yield savings equivalent to 1 percent of GDP a year.

The reform project involves evaluating and motivating managers by means of a "signaling system." The system will have three components:

(1) setting clear and reasonable goals for managers

(2) measuring actual performance

(3) rewarding managers according to how well they achieved

their goals

(1) Setting Clear and Reasonable Goals

The fundamental difficulties in setting targets against which SOE performance can be measured are the lack of agreement about what the

---

1/ This section is based on work by Leroy P. Jones (Boston University) for WDR VI as well as Jones, "Toward a Performance Evaluation Methodology for Public Enterprises with Special Reference to Pakistan," paper presented to the International Symposium on Economic Performance of Public Enterprises (Islamabad, November 24-28, 1981), background information and comments from Ian Banon (World Bank), and World Bank files. See also Jones, "Efficiency of Public Manufacturing Enterprises in Pakistan," (paper prepared for the World Bank and the Ministry of Production of Pakistan, August 1981; processed).

objectives are and how they should be weighted, and the impossibility of quantifying some of these goals. The signaling system approaches these problems by separating commercial from noncommercial goals. Commercial objectives can be quantified, and--with some adjustments--profit provides a composite indicator of performance in minimizing costs and maximizing benefits. There is high-level support in Pakistan for requiring SOEs to operate as efficiently as possible.

The primary indicator of commercial performance will be "public profits," which are private profits adjusted for those elements that are not deemed relevant for an SOE. For example, taxes and interest, which are private costs but public benefits, are excluded so as not to encourage SOE managers to devote time to minimizing taxes or to interest arbitrage. Rather, public profitability aims to encourage managers to maximize net economic benefits, judged from a national perspective.

The thorny problem of noncommercial objectives remains, of course. The system does not yet provide for evaluating the achievement of these objectives. Fortunately, many of these goals are met by the very existence of the firm-- for example, national control over certain sectors or the opening up of backward areas. The cost of these goals may be reflected in a lower level of public profits, but the operational goal will still be to maximize those profits. Since performance is measured by the trend in a firm's public profitability, the cost of these noncommercial objectives will not affect results.

Some noncommercial objectives have a varying effect on the trend in profits, however, and this must be explicitly taken into account. Under the signaling system, the cost of meeting such objectives (for example, the extra cost of purchasing from local suppliers to encourage domestic industry) are negotiated between the government and the SOE, deducted before profits are calculated, and treated as an "in-kind" dividend to the government. These calculations must be carefully done since, if the adjustment is set too high, managers' incentive to minimize cost is reduced. If it is set too low, the SOE will be unfairly evaluated and the credibility of the system will suffer. A proposed "disclosure bonus" system (see below) may reduce these risks.

(2) Measuring Actual Performance

In terms of a standard profit and loss statement, public profit consists of:

+ sales
- inventory changes
- manufacturing costs
- administrative and selling costs
- total employee costs
+ depreciation and amortization allowances
- opportunity cost of working capital.

This information can be gathered from standard financial statements.

Since many prices are administered in Pakistan and there are problems of monopoly pricing, market prices may not reflect true economic scarcity. Since SOE managers generally cannot affect prices, it would be unfair to reward or penalize them for the effects of changing prices on profitability. The ideal solution would be to eliminate the divergence between market prices and real economic costs. Where that is not feasible, a second best remedy is to use shadow prices that do reflect true economic costs. However, shadow prices are complex and controversial to administer. Pakistan is therefore judging those SOE managers facing administered prices, for control purposes only, by trends in public profit at constant prices. That is the equivalent of constructing a quantum index of profits based on quantum indices of inputs and outputs. This is an acceptable approximation of efficiency in performance evaluation (though not in project evaluation), to the extent that performance evaluation concentrates on the trend rather than the level of performance. The enterprises will be judged on the basis of their return to fixed operating assets, or public profitability in constant terms. (SOEs which are free to set their own prices will be evaluated by public profitability in current terms.) The performance of any individual firm will be compared with its own record over the past five years, to make allowance for the fact that some enterprises operate under greater handicaps than others. The profitability trend may be supplemented by comparisons with similar firms in Pakistan or elsewhere and by expert judgments to arrive at a suitable target for each company. Thus a poorly situated enterprise might receive a top score for moving from a -10 percent loss to -5 percent, while a more fortunate SOE might receive a poor score for a 25 percent profit if last year it has earned a 35 percent profit.

To induce managers to give their best estimate of enterprise potential, a disclosure bonus scheme can also be used. Under such a scheme, the ministry sets a target and an associated bonus level. The SOE is free to adjust the target--the bonus is adjusted in the same direction by an adjustment formula. The final bonus is then adjusted for both over-and under-fulfillment of the target in such a way as to give the highest bonus for both top performance and setting a realistic target. 2/

2/ See L. Jones, "Towards a Performance Evaluation Methodology for Public Enterprises with Special Reference to Pakistan" pp. 24-27 for details.

Used in isolation, public profitability would encourage managers to ignore activities with current costs but future benefits (such as planning, maintenance, training, or innovation). The government and the SOEs therefore negotiate extra targets for these areas, assigning them weights which vary over time and from one company to another. A firm will first have to show that it can use existing resources efficiently; hence, 90 percent of its initial target may be assigned to public profitability, later this may drop to perhaps 70 percent.

(3) Rewarding managers according to how well they achieved their goals

At the end of each year, an SOE's performance will be rated according to how close it came to meeting its composite target. The monitoring and evaluation will be done by the Experts Advisory Cell, a semi-autonomous agency responsible to the Ministry of Production but financed by a levy on the SOEs themselves. The cell has been able to maintain a remarkable degree of independence and, because it is outside the civil service pay system, to attract a specialist staff. At a review meeting with the Cell, managers will be able to present an explanation of their results. The manager's performance would then be rated, taking into account circumstances beyond management's control. In addition to the incentive provided by public recognition of performance, it is proposed that managers and employees receive a bonus of so many months' pay depending on the performance rating. It is expected that good performance will also be rewarded by greater autonomy and poor performance penalized by reduced independence, although this is not formally part of the system.

Experience to Date

The design of the system is an iterative process. In 1982 prototype evaluation and information systems were tried and then modified after full discussions with managers and ministry officials. The SOE and ministry staff were trained in supplying and processing the information. The information system was based primarily on standard (though detailed) financial statements routinely produced by the SOEs, plus price and quality data available, though not regularly reported. A few days' work at each enterprise is usually sufficient to collect data for a five-year historical period. The data are then computerized and can be used to generate reports outside the signaling system--eliminating repetitive requests for information from the enterprises.

The information system covering 60 units began operating in January 1983, greatly improving the quality and timeliness of information on SOE performance. The evaluation system is expected to be in place by mid-summer, 1983. All SOEs will be required to submit detailed budget plans for the next fiscal year (covering employment, inputs, production, sales, profits, and the like) as a basis for negotiating performance targets. The incentive scheme is still being decided.

Conclusions

Although it is too early to judge the outcome of the project, some tentative conclusions can be drawn. The project has already served to focus attention on SOE efficiency and to generate considerable data that will allow the Ministry of Production to assess the aggregate impact of its SOEs. The establishment of the Experts Advisory Cell has also been important in attracting new expertise and creating a precedent for a semiautonomous unit outside the government pay limitations.

Of course, the real test of the signaling system--negotiating targets and evaluating performance--has yet to come. The degree of high level political commitment and the professionalism of the Advisory Cell bode well for the future of the project, as does the emphasis on negotiation with the SOE managers.

If it operates properly, the signaling system should work both ways --notifying managers about what the state expects of them and also signaling the government when its demands are unreasonable. It should thus pressure managers to improve SOE performance and also pressure government to take policy decisions to allow the firms to meet their targets. For example, if an SOE falls short of a target because of delays caused by bureaucratic red tape or high costs caused by a rise in administered prices or labor policies, management has a strong incentive to complain and demand an adjustment. This brings the problem--and the cost--out into the open. Ideally, this would result in a gradual process of successive reforms on the part of both government and enterprise.

The signaling system is not meant to operate in isolation. Measures to increase SOE autonomy and upgrade managerial skills are clearly integral to its success. Furthermore, since it concentrates on trends (not levels) of profits, assessments of the economic return on government investment will be needed to determine whether some enterprises might not best be liquidated, as well as to decide on new investments.

Statistical Appendix

Table 1 Nonfinancial SOE Shares in GDP at Factor Cost
(percentages)

Industrialized countries

France (1983)	17.0 a/	Italy (1978)	7.5 a/
Austria (1978–79)	14.5 a/	Ireland (1982)	8.0
United Kingdom (1978–81)	10.9 d/	Denmark (1974)	6.3
Fed. Rep. of Germany (1979)	1.0	Spain (1979)	4.1 a/
Australia (1978)	9.4 e/	Netherlands (1971–73)	3.6

Developing countries

Algeria (1978)	66.0	Portugal (1976)	9.7
Hungary (1980)	63.5 b/	Kenya (1970–73)	8.7
Zambia (1972)	37.8	Argentina (1975)	8.6
Guyana (1978–80)	37.2	Benin (1976)	7.6 a/
Nicaragua (1980)	36.0	Sierra Leone (1979)	7.6
Egypt (1977)	31.4	Mexico (1978)	7.4 c/
Venezuela (1978–80)	27.5 a/	Botswana (1978–79)	7.3 a/
Tunisia (1978–79)	25.4	Liberia (1977)	6.8
Guinea (1979)	25.0 a/	Korea (1974–77)	6.4
Senegal (1974)	19.9 a/	Greece (1979)	6.1
Chile (1982)	17.7	Pakistan (1974–75)	6.0
Tanzania (1974–77)	12.3	Bangladesh (1974)	5.7
Bolivia (1974–77)	12.1 a/	Mali (1978)	5.2 a/
Togo (1980)	11.8	Turkey (1978–80)	5.0 a/
Ivory Coast (1979)	10.5 a/	Thailand (1970–73)	3.6
India (1978)	10.3	Paraguay (1978–80)	3.1 a/
Sri Lanka (1974)	9.9	Nepal (1978–79)	3.0
Mali (1978)	9.4 c/	Philippines (1974–77)	1.7

---

a/ Share in GDP at market cost.
b/ Excludes cooperatives.
c/ Major enterprises only.
d/ Includes financial enterprises.
e/ Includes some local enterprises.

coverage: Where possible the figures are for majority owned, national
enterprises whose output is sold and is of a type where
revenue is expected to cover a substantial part of costs.

Sources: Peter Short, UNIDO, IIAS, and Bank files.

Table 2 National Nonfinancial SOE Shares in Gross Fixed
Capital Formation
(percentage)

Developed countries

Norway (1978-80)	22.2	France (1978-81)	12.1
Austria (1978-79)	19.2	Ireland (1978)	11.8
United Kingdom (1978-81)	17.0	Sweden (1978-80)	11.4
Spain (1978-80)	15.6	Japan (1978-80)	11.4 a/
Italy (1979-80)	15.2	Germany (1978-79)	10.8
Belgium (1978-79)	13.1	United States (1978)	4.4 a/
Netherlands (1978)	12.6 a/	Canada (1978-80)	2.7

Developing countries

Algeria (1978-81)	67.6	Sierre Leone (1979)	19.6
Zambia (1979-80)	61.2	Argentina (1978-80)	19.6 b/
Burma (1978-80)	60.6	Costa Rica (1977-79)	19.6
Egypt (1976-79)	47.8	Uruguay (1978-80)	18.3
Pakistan (1978-81)	44.6	Senegal (1974)	17.9
Bolivia (1974-77)	40.9	Kenya (1978-79)	17.3
Ivory Coast (1979)	39.5	Tanzania (1978-79)	16.3
Gambia (1978-80)	37.9	Peru (1978-79)	14.8
Mauritania (1978-79)	37.2	Honduras (1978-79)	14.6
Ethiopia (1978-80)	36.5	Mauritius (1977-79)	14.4
Venezuela (1978-80)	36.3	Liberia (1977)	14.1
Tunisia (1980-81)	35.8	Guatemala (1978-80)	13.3
Guyana (1978-80)	35.1	Chile (1978-80)	12.9 b/
India (1978)	33.7	Thailand (1978-79)	12.8
Portugal (1978-80)	33.2 a/ e/	Haiti (1978-80)	12.4 a/ b/
Bahamas (1978-79)	31.6	Philippines (1978)	10.9 a/
Bangladesh (1974)	31.0	Greece (1979)	8.7 a/
Mexico (1978)	29.4	Dominican Republic (1978-79)	8.4 b/
Sri Lanka (1978)	28.4	Dominica (1978-79)	7.8
Panama	27.7 a/	Botswana (1978-79)	7.7
Turkey	27.5 f/	Mali (1978)	7.6 b/
Jamaica (1978-80)	24.8 a/ b/	St. Lucia (1978-79)	6.7
Brazil (1980)	22.8	Paraguay (1978-80)	6.5
Korea (1978-80)	22.8 a/	Malta (1978-80)	6.3 c/
Malawi (1978)	21.2	Colombia (1978-80)	5.6

Weighted Average d/	
Industrial countries	11.1
Developing countries	27.0

---

a/	Share in gross capital formation (including stocks).
b/	Major enterprises only.
c/	Excluding industrial enterprises.
d/	Weighted average for 1974-77 using gross fixed capital formation formation at market prices.
e/	Includes financial enterprises.
f/	State economic enterprises only.

Sources and coverage: see table 1

Table 3 Nonfinancial SOE Shares of Nonagricultural and Public Sector Employment
(percent)

	Nonagricultural Employment	Public Sector Employment
Australia (1980)	2.8	10.4
Belgium (1980)	7.5	23.0
Canada (1981)	3.3	20.3
Denmark (1981)	2.6	9.4
Germany (1980)	4.2	21.3
Iceland (1980)	2.8	16.2
Ireland (1978)	8.8	32.9
Italy (1980)	2.5	12.6
Japan (1980)	1.6	15.6
Netherlands (1980)	1.1	5.6
New Zealand (1981)	6.9	19.0
Sweden (1979)	3.4	10.1
United Kingdom (1980)	8.5	27.6
United States (1981)	0.7	3.6
AFRICA		
Benin (1979)	37.1	42.7
Kenya (1980)	8.4	21.5
Liberia (1982)	6.9	11.5
Mauritius (1980)	14.2	26.9
Senegal (1976)	12.9	28.2
Swaziland (1982)	1.8	7.5
Tanzania (1978)	31.9	40.8
Zambia (1980)	36.5	45.0
LATIN AMERICA		
Argentina (1981)	4.5	19.7
Bahamas (1978)	16.0	13.9
Barbados (1981)	24.1	n.a.
Guatemala (1981)	15.9	5.6
Jamaica (1980)	23.4	n.a.
Panama (1979)	19.3	34.9
St. Lucia (1981)	28.3	n.a.
ASIA		
India (1977)	17.7	24.5
Korea (1981)	2.5	15.8
Philippines (1979)	14.0	52.6
Sri Lanka (1980)	28.7	63.0
NORTH AFRICA		
Egypt (1979)	10.3	26.0

Source: Heller and Tait (forthcoming)

Bibliography

Amouyel, P. "Contractural Relations between the State and the Public Sector: The French Experience with Contracts concluded with Public Enterprises." Draft background paper prepared for the World Bank, November 12, 1982 (original: French).

Basu, P.K., and Alex Nove. Public Enterprise Policy on Investment, Pricing, Returns. Kuala Lumpur: Asian and Pacific Development Administration Center, 1979.

Baumol, William T., ed. Public and Private Enterprise in A Mixed Economy. New York: St. Martin's, 1980.

Brazil, Planning Secretariat. Secretariat for Control of State Enterprises, State Enterprises in Brazil and the Control of the SEST: Background and 1980 Results. Brazilia, 1981.

Caves, D. W., and L. R. Christensen. "The Relative Efficiency of Public and Private Firms in a Competitive Environment: The Case of Canadian Railways." Journal of Political Economy (October, 1980).

Choski, Armeane M. State Intervention in the Industrialization of Developing Countries: Selected Issues. World Bank Staff Working Paper no. 341. Washington, D.C , 1979.

Covian, General Don Luis, and Enrique Matte Voras. Presentation to the Seminar on Public Enterprises. Brazil, September 1982.

Davis, D. G. "The Efficiency of Public versus Private Firms: The Case of Australia's Two Airlines." Journal of Law and Economics (April, 1971).

Feibel, Charles, and A. A. Walters. "Ownership and Efficiency in Urban Buses." September 1979. Processed.

Fernandes, P., ed. Control Systems for Public Enterprises in Developing Countries. (Ljubljana, Yugoslavia, 1982).

Gantt, A., and G. Dutto. "Financial Performance of Government-owned Corporations in Less Developed Countries." International Monetary Fund Staff Working Papers, vol. 25, 1968, pp. 102-142.

Gordon, David. Development Finance Companies, State and Privately Owned: A Review. World Bank Staff Working Paper no. 578. Washington, D.C., 1983.

Hibbs, John. "Urban Bus Transport in Buenos Aires--The 'Colectivos'" N.d. Processed.

Heller, Peter, and Allen Tait. "Government Employment and Pay: Some International Comparisons." Forthcoming in the IMF Occasional Paper series.

India, Bureau of Public Enterprises. "Performance Aims and Financial Targets of Central Government Public Enterprises, 1982/83 and 1983/84." New Delhi, 1982.

_____. Public Enterprise Survey, 1980-81. Vol. I-III. New Delhi, 1982.

Jones, Leroy P. "Definition and Taxonomy of Public Enterprise." In Seeking the Personality of the Public Enterprise. Edited by P. Fernandes ICPE, 1981.

_____. "Efficiency of Public Manufacturing Enterprises in Pakistan." Paper prepared for the World Bank and the Ministry of Production of Pakistan, August 1981. Processed.

_____. Public Enterprise in Less Developed Countries. Cambridge: Cambridge University Press, 1982.

_____. Public Enterprise for Whom? Perverse Distributional Consequences of Public Operational Decisions." Paper read at the Conference of Problems and Policies of Industrialization in an Open Economy, at Bogazici University, Istanbul, Turkey, August 20-24, 1981.

_____. "Towards a Performance Evaluation Methodology for Public Enterprises with Special References to Pakistan." Paper for U.N. International Symposium in Pakistan, 1981.

Kenya. Report and Recommendations of the Working Party on Government Expenditues (Philip Ndegwa, Chairman), July, 1982.

Khandwalla, Pradip N. "Performance Determinants of Public Enterprises: Case Studies of Four Equipment Manufacturing Indian Public Enterprises." Vols. 1-3. World Bank Staff Working Paper (forthcoming).

Knight, Peter. Economic Reforms in Socialist Countries: The Experiences of China, Hungary, Romania and Yugoslavia. World Bank Staff Working Paper no. 586. Washington, D.C , 1983.

Krueger, Anne O., and Baran Tuncer. Estimating Total Factor Productivity Growth. World Bank Staff Working Paper no. 422. Washington, D.C., October 1980.

Lamb, Geoffrey, and Linda Muller. Control, Accountability, and Incentives in a Successful Development Institution: The Kenya Tea Development Authority. World Bank Staff Working Paper no. 550. Washington, D.C., 1982.

Meyer, Robert A. "Publicly Owned versus Privately Owned Utilities: A Policy Choice." The Review of Economics and Statistics, Vol. LVII, No. 4, November, 1975.

Munasinghe, M., and J. Warford. Electricity Pricing: Theory and Case Studies. Baltimore: Johns Hopkins University Press, 1982.

Prodi, Romano. "Economic Performance and Political Problems of Public Industrial Firms in Italy." World Bank Staff Working Paper (forthcoming).

Redwood, John. Public Enterprise in Crisis. Oxford: Basil Blackwell, 1980.

Redwood, John, and John Hatch. Controlling Public Industries. Oxford: Basil Blackwell, 1982.

_____. Value for Money Audits. London: Center for Policy Studies, 1981.

Roth, Gabriel, and George G. Wynne. Learning From Abroad, Free Enterprise Urban Transportation. New Brunswick, N.J.: Transaction Books, 1982.

Sadique, A.S., ed. Public Enterprise in Asia: Studies on Coordination and Control. Kuala Lumpur, Asian Center for Development Administration, 1976.

Schrenk, M. Managerial Structures and Practices in Manufacturing Enterprises: A Yugoslav Case Study. World Bank Staff Working Paper no. 455, May 1981.

Sheahan, John. Differences in the Roles and Consequences of Public Enterprise in Developing Countries. Williamstown, Mass.: Williams College, Research Memorandum Series, 1981.

Shepherd, W. G. and Associates. Public Enterprise: Economic Analysis of Theory and Practice. Lexington, Mass.: Lexington Books, 1978.

Short, Peter. "Appraising the Role of Public Enterprises, an International Comparison." IMF Occasional Paper Series, Washington, D.C , 1983.

"The State in the Market." The Economist, December 30, 1978.

UNIDO, Ahmad, Muzaffer. "Organizational Framework, Institutional Relations and Management of Public Industrial Enterprises." October 1981.

UNIDO, Ansari, T.A. "Comparative Study of Impact of Public and Private Manufacturing Sectors in Selected Developing Countries." October 1981.

UNIDO, ECWA Secretariat. "The Public Enterprises and Industrialization in ECWA Region." October 1981.

UNIDO, ESCAP Secretariat. "Public Enterprises and Industrialization in ESCAP Countries." October 1981.

UNIDO, Killick, T. "The Role of the Public Sector in the Industrialization of African Developing Countries." October 1981.

UNIDO, Roman, Z. "The Role and Function of the Public Sector in Industrial Development in the European Centrally Planned Economies." October 1981.

UNIDO Secretariat. "Changing Role and Function of the Public Industrial Sector in Developing Countries." October 1981.

United Kingdom. The Financial and Economic Obligations of the Nationalized Industries. London, April 1961.

United Kingdom Commonwealth Secretariat. National Policies and Programs for Public Enterprise Management Training. London, 1979.

_____. Issues in Public Enterprise Development. London, 1978.

_____. Financing of the Nationalized Industries. Eighth Report from the Treasury and Civil Service Committee, Session 1980-81. London, 27 July 1981.

United Kingdom, House of Commons. Parliaments, Governments and Public Enterprises. London, undated.

Vernon, Raymond, and Yair Aharoui, eds. State-Owned Enterprise in the Western Economies. New York: St. Martin's Press, 1981.

Walstedt, B. State Manufacturing Enterprise in a Mixed Economy: The Turkish Case. Baltimore: Johns Hopkins University Press, 1980.

Walters, A. A. Costs and Scale of Bus Services. World Bank Staff Working Paper no. 325. Washington, D.C., April, 1979.

Windle, R., and W. Keyser, eds. Public Enterprise in the EEC. 7 vols. Sythoff and Nordhoff, 1978.

Williams, David. "The Choice of Technology and National Planning: The Case of Tanzania." Unpublished DBA thesis, Harvard University Graduate School of Business Administration, 1975.

World Bank. "Arab Republic of Egypt: Issues of Trade Strategy and Investment Planning." Washington, D.C , January 14, 1983. Restricted circulation document for internal use only.

_____. "Chile: Economic Memorandum." Washington, D.C., September 28, 1981. Restricted circulation document for internal use only.

_____. "The Railways Problem." Washington, D.C., January 28, 1982. Restricted circulation document for internal use only.

_____. "Turkey: Industrialization and Trade Strategy." Washington, D.C., February 18, 1983. Restricted circulation document for internal use only.

_____. "Turkey: Issues and Options in the Energy Sector." Washington, D.C., March, 1983. Restricted circulation document for internal use only.

World Bank and IFC. "Peru: The Management and Sale of State-owned Enterprises." Washington, D.C , August 27, 1982. Restricted circulation document for internal use only.

The World Bank
Publications Order Form

SEND TO: **YOUR LOCAL DISTRIBUTOR** OR TO **WORLD BANK PUBLICATIONS**
(See the other side of this form.) P.O. BOX 37525
WASHINGTON, D.C. 20013 U.S.A.

Date _____

Name _____

Title _____

Firm _____

Address _____

City _____ State_____ Postal Code_____

Country _____ Telephone (_____) _____

Purchaser Reference No. _____

Ship to: (Enter if different from purchaser)

Name _____

Title _____

Firm _____

Address _____

City _____ State_____ Postal Code_____

Country _____ Telephone (_____) _____

Check your method of payment.
Enclosed is my ☐ Check ☐ International Money Order ☐ Unesco Coupons ☐ International Postal Coupon.
Make payable to World Bank Publications for U.S. dollars unless you are ordering from your local distributor.

Charge my ☐ VISA ☐ MasterCard ☐ American Express ☐ Choice. (Credit cards accepted only for orders addressed to World Bank Publications.)

_____   _____   _____
Credit Card Account Number   Expiration Date   Signature

☐ Invoice me and please reference my Purchase Order No. _____.

Please ship me the items listed below.

Stock Number	Author/ Title	Customer Internal Routing Code	Quantity	Unit Price	Total Amount $

All prices subject to change.   Prices may vary by country.   Allow 6–8 weeks for delivery.

Subtotal Cost $_____

Total copies _____ Air mail surcharge if desired ($2.00 each) $_____

Postage and handling for more than two complimentary items ($2.00 each) $_____

Total $_____

IBRD-0053   **Thank you for your order.**

DISTRIBUTORS OF WORLD BANK PUBLICATIONS

ALGERIA
Office des Publications Universitaires
1, place centrale de Ben-Aknoun
Algiers

ARGENTINA
Carlos Hirsch, SRL
Galeria Guemes
Florida 165, 4th Floor-Ofc. 453/465
1333 Buenos Aires

**AUSTRALIA, PAPUA NEW GUINEA, FIJI
SOLOMON ISLANDS, AND VANUATU**
Info-Line
Overseas Document Delivery
Box 506, GPO
Sydney, NSW 2001

AUSTRIA
Gerold and Co.
A-1011 Wien
Graben 31

BAHRAIN
MEMRB
P.O. Box 22103
Manama Town 317

BANGLADESH
Micro Industries Development
   Assistance Society (MIDAS)
G.P.O. Box 800
Dhaka

BELGIUM
Publications des Nations Unies
Av. du Roi 202
1060 Brussels

BRAZIL
Publicacoes Tecnicas Internacionais Ltda.
Rua Peixoto Gomide, 209
01409 Sao Paulo, SP

CANADA
Le Diffuseur
C.P. 85, 1501 Ampere Street
Boucherville, Quebec
J4B 5E6

CHILE
Editorial Renacimiento
Miraflores 354
Santiago

COLOMBIA
Enlace Ltda.
Apartado Aereo 34270
Bogota D.E.

Apartado Aereo 4430
Cali, Valle

COSTA RICA
Libreria Trejos
Calle 11-13
Av. Fernandez Guell
San Jose

CYPRUS
MEMRB
P.O. Box 2098
Nicosia

DENMARK
SamfundsLitteratur
Rosenoerns Alle 11
DK-1970 Copenhagen V

EGYPT, ARAB REPUBLIC OF
Al Ahram
Galaa Street
Cairo

FINLAND
Akateeminen Kirjakauppa
P.O. Box 128
SF-00101
Helsinki 10

FRANCE
World Bank Publications
66, avenue d'Iena
75116 Paris

GERMANY, FEDERAL REPUBLIC OF
UNO-Verlag
D-5300 Bonn 1
Simrockstrasse 23

GREECE
MEMRB
24, Ippodamou Street
Athens-11635

HONG KONG, MACAU
Asia 2000 Ltd.
6 Fl., 146 Prince Edward Road, W,
Kowloon
Hong Kong

HUNGARY
Kultura
H-1011 Budapest
Fioi Utca 32

INDIA
UBS Publishers' Distributors Ltd.
Post Box 7015
New Delhi 110002

10 First Main Road
Gandhi Nagar
Bangalore 560009

Apeejay Chambers, P.O. Box 736
5 Wallace Street
Bombay 400001

8/1-B, Chowringhee Lane
Calcutta 700016

7/188, 1(CA), Swarup Nagar
Kampu 208002

Sivaganga Road
Nungambakkam
Madras 600034

INDONESIA
Pt. Indira Limited
Jl. Sam Ratulangi 37
Jakarta Pusat
P.O. Box 181

IRELAND
TDC Publishers
12 North Frederick Street
Dublin 1

ISRAEL
Jerusalem Post
Jerusalem Post Building
P.O. Box 81
Romema Jerusalem 91000

ITALY
Licosa Commissionaria Sansoni SPA
Via Lamarmora 45
Casella Postale 552
50121 Florence

IVORY COAST
Centre d'Edition et de Diffusion
   Africaines (CEDA)
04 B.P. 541
Abidjan 04 Plateau

JAPAN
Eastern Book Service
37-3, Hongo 3-Chome, Bunkyo-ku 113
Tokyo

JORDAN
MEMRB
P.O. Box 3143
Jabal
Amman

KENYA
Africa Book Service (E.A.) Ltd.
P.O. Box 45245
Nairobi

KOREA, REPUBLIC OF
Pan Korea Book Corporation
P.O. Box 101, Kwangwhamun
Seoul

KUWAIT
MEMRB
P.O. Box 5465

MALAYSIA
University of Malaya
   Cooperative Bookshop, Limited
P.O. Box 1127, Jalan Pantai Baru
Kuala Lumpur

MEXICO
INFOTEC
San Lorenzo 153-11. Col. del Valle
   Deleg. Benito Juarez
03100 Mexico City

MOROCCO
MEMRB
2 Rue Moliere Racine
Casablanca

NETHERLANDS
Medical Books Europe, BV (MBE)
Noorderwal 38,
7241 BL Lochem

NEW ZEALAND
R. Hill and Son, Ltd.
Private Bag
New Market
Auckland

NIGERIA
University Press Limited
Three Crowns Building Jericho
Private Mail Bag 5095
Ibadan

NORWAY
Tanum Karl Johan, A.S.
P.O. Box 1177 Sentrum
Oslo 1

PAKISTAN
Mirza Book Agency
65, Shahrah-e-Quaid-e-Azam
P.O. Box No. 729
Lahore 3

PANAMA
Ediciones Librena Cultural
Panamena, S.A.
Av. 7, Espana 16
Panama Zone 1

PERU
Editorial Desarrollo SA
Apartado 3824
Lima

PHILIPPINES
National Book Store
701 Rizal Avenue
Metro Manila

PORTUGAL
Livrana Portugal
Rua Do Carmo 70-74
1200 Lisbon

SAUDI ARABIA
Jarir Book Store
P.O. Box 3196
Riyadh 11471

SINGAPORE, TAIWAN, BURMA
Information Publications
Private. Ltd.
02-06 1st Fl., Pei-Fu Industrial
Bldg., 24 New Industrial Road
Singapore

SOUTH AFRICA
Oxford University Press Southern Africa
P.O. Box 1141
Cape Town 8000

SPAIN
Mundi-Prensa Libros, S.A.
Castello 37
28001 Madrid

SRI LANKA AND THE MALDIVES
Lake House Bookshop
P.O. Box 244
100, Sir Chittampalam A.
   Gardiner Mawatha
Colombo 2

SWEDEN
For single titles:
ABCE Fritzes Kungl. Hovbokhandel
Attn: Mr. Eide Segerback
Regeringsgatan 12, Box 16356
S-103 27 Stockholm

For subscription orders:
Wennergren-Williams AB
Box 30004
S-104 25 Stockholm

SWITZERLAND
Librairie Payot
6 Rue Grenus
Case postal 381
CH 1211 Geneva 11

TANZANIA
Oxford University Press
P.O. Box 5299
Dar es Salaam

THAILAND
Central Department Store
306 Silom Road
Bangkok

TRINIDAD & TOBAGO
Systematics Studies Unit
55 Eastern Main Road
Curepe
Trinidad, West Indies

TUNISIA
Societe Tunisienne de Diffusion
5 Avenue de Carthage
Tunis

TURKEY
Haset Kitapevi A.S.
469, Istiklal Caddesi
Beyoglu-Istanbul

UGANDA
Uganda Bookshop
P.O. Box 7145
Kampala

UNITED ARAB EMIRATES
MEMRB
P.O. Box 6097
Sharjah

**UNITED KINGDOM
AND NORTHERN IRELAND**
Microinfo Ltd.
P.O. Box 3
Alton, Hampshire GU 34 2PG
England

VENEZUELA
Librena del Este
Aptdo. 60.337
Caracas 1060-A

WESTERN SAMOA
Wesley Bookshop
P.O. Box 207
Apia

ZIMBABWE
Textbook Sales Pvt. Ltd.
Box 3799
Harare